Do Not Sit

A Journey to Wholeness

BY TRINA RODRIGUEZ

SKINNY BROWN DOG
MEDIA
EST. 2013
ATLANTA | PUNTA DEL ESTE

Distributed by Skinny Brown Dog Media

Design and composition by Skinny Brown Dog Media

Cover Design by Skinny Brown Dog Media

Interior Layout Design by farhanshahid101

Library of Congress Cataloging-in-Publication Data Print

Do Not Sit - A Journey to Wholeness

eBook ISBN: 978-1-957506-43-2

Hardback ISBN: 978-1-957506-45-6

Paperback ISBN: 978-1-957506-44-9

Do Not Sit

I couldn't wait to be forty years old. Forty was my magic number. It meant my youngest child was eighteen years old and I had reached a pinnacle time in my life. I was excited about the possibility of traveling, going on new adventures, taking risks, and living life to the fullest. I was eager and ready to experience new things beginning with the purchase of my brand-new motorcycle. My biggest birthday surprise was that my sister Missy drove down from Baltimore to celebrate my big day!!

We played cards, took turns riding my motorcycle, and just enjoying each other's company. The weekend was a success and I felt energized and ready to begin my new life after forty. Still, Sunday seemed to come too soon and my sister, her son Karl, and my daughter Queen had to leave. I was sad that they had to go but Missy's presence really made my fortieth birthday my best birthday ever!!

The following Friday, as I was preparing to go to work, I received a phone call. On the other end was my nephew Karl sobbing uncontrollably and mumbling words I couldn't understand.

As I urged him to calm down, I heard Queen's voice in the background stammering something about an ambulance and having to resuscitate my sister. I was confused, helpless, and scared but I knew one thing...I had to get to Missy. She needed me and I was five hours away. I hung up the phone, my husband and I gathered our bags, collected my youngest daughter, and headed to...Baltimore, not sure what was going on.

Once we were in the car I called my job to tell them what was happening and that I would be out of the office for a while. As I was on a call with my boss, my husband started to nudge me to get off the phone and saying he needed to speak to me. I brushed him off and told him I...was trying to talk to my office and he needed to give me a minute. He said, "Honey, I really need to talk to you, can you hang up the phone?" I finally conceded and told my boss I would call her later with updates. I turned to him and asked him, "What is it that you need, what is sooo important?" He took a really slow breath and said "Your sister has died." Everything went silent. I could only hear the pounding in my chest. What do you mean my sister has died? She was just here last week, she can't be gone, not gone forever. Then all of a sudden, I let out a blood curdling scream that jolted me out of darkness into reality. My sister had died!!!

This drive was the slowest most miserable journey of my life. Missy was more than just my sister...she was my mother, my friend, my confidant. She was literally everything I knew about myself! She was gone and I was lost. I kept hearing her voice when she called me earlier in the week telling me how she was feeling sick and her supervisor had threatened...to write her up if she didn't come in. So she went. Just three days before her death and she went to work anyway. I keep thinking why would she go to work sick, why didn't she care more about her health rather than a damn job!!

When I got to the hospital in Baltimore I learned that Missy died of sudden cardiac arrest.

They allowed me one last glance before they covered her with a sheet. She meant so much to me. It was so hard to let go. The next few days I had the difficult task of preparing for her funeral and the process was mentally and physically draining but I made it through. Then I had to take care of one more thing...I had to go to her job to collect her belongings.

Missy's supervisor greeted me at the entrance and escorted me back to her desk. It was a completely open space that was dimly lit and felt really cold. In the center of the room was a lone chair that had a sign affixed to it that read... DO NOT SIT! Those words pierced me like...a spear through my heart. My sister had spent 20 years working for this company, sitting in that chair for most of it and that was all that what was left of her? A sign that the company affixed to a chair! Was that all her sacrificing was for? A stupid sign? Was that the entire legacy that she left? I had no answers for her life! And in that moment, I realized, I had no answers for my own.

During the drive home I was emotionally bankrupt and all I kept seeing was the vision of that sign in that chair. I could not get it out of my head. It seemed to have imprinted my soul! DO...NOT SIT! And that's when I decided that I didn't want to be in the passenger seat of my life any longer. I did not want my sister's fate to be my fate. So instead of sitting, I decided to stand and DO NOT SIT became my motivation to keep moving and not to sit, not even one more day! I want to be counted. I want to be heard.

So today I plead with you!!

- ☒ DO NOT SIT and waste the talents you have been given!

- ☒ DO NOT SIT around and expect someone to hand you your dreams!

- ☒ DO NOT SIT out on opportunities to be better!

- ☒ DO NOT SIT and wait for your life to pass you by!

Contents

Dedication

In memory of my mother and my sister, Missy. Your presence in my life taught me to stand and never sit. I miss you both with every fiber of my being!

Acknowledgments

There are not enough words to communicate how much love, support, and guidance Ann and Anyssa have given me throughout this process.

Through countless hours of journaling sessions with Ann and Anyssa's commitment to reading and editing each and every story, together they made this book a reality.

You two are the greatest.

Thank you!

A Note From a Friend

I don't remember how Trina and I started writing together. I'm just glad that we did. At first, we were work colleagues, and then suddenly, we were writing buddies. Every weekday morning during "the Covid times," we met virtually at 8 am, wrote for twenty minutes, and shared our writing and, in the process, our lives.

Trina's writings were always vibrant and full of details that carried you away. Her descriptions brought you into the story so that you felt it was your story and she was the narrator. She has a way of pulling you into her writing so you feel you are there.

Her writings which you are about to read, will draw you in like a big, comfy chair and will provide you with luscious, colorful food for thought. I know reading her stories will motivate you to write your own. I hope you enjoy your journey!

Ann Roy

Letter From The Author

Dear Reader,

We are here today because I promised myself that my life would not be a book never written or a story never told. What I mean by that is that each of us has a gift or a light that we are meant to share, but far too often, we are convinced that what we have isn't special, worthy, or valuable. So here I am, pouring my heart out to the world, sharing my light and my gift with you. Would you believe it if I told you that prior to this book, I had never considered myself a writer? However, after I committed myself to writing in my journal for twenty minutes a day, a writer is what I became, and this book is the result.

On this journey to wholeness, I have asked myself many questions along the way. Who am I? Why was I born? How did I end up where I am today? I have reminisced and written my most heartfelt stories, and in return, they have given me a deep appreciation for the unique person that I have become. What you will read in this book is my JOURNAL, meaning my **J**ourney **O**f **U**nconditional, **R**eflection, **N**ecessary, (for) **A**udacious **L**iving. It is full of stories that have revealed deep pain, grief, reflection, aha moments, self-acceptance, love, and living out loud. I would have never believed I had so much inside me until I decided to write freely and unapologetically. Most importantly, this journey has taught me that life often yields more questions than answers, and that's okay.

Sometimes things in life are inexplicable. Sometimes things are made to be forgotten. However, most experiences are made to be shared for laughter, for lessons, and as a means of connection to know that you are not alone in your lived experience. As I look back at my own life, I know that there are many people struggling to answer the same questions that I asked of myself. This book speaks to all of them. It is my hope that this book will speak to your heart and give you the courage to step into your journey of self-acceptance, self-love, and self-awareness.

I hope you enjoy my stories and learn to appreciate your own!

With much love and appreciation,

Trina

Omit

There are many times I choose to omit part of my story.

I wonder if I do that subconsciously or intentionally. It seems whenever I get to the hard parts of my story, I don't want to tell it. I know that people can learn or be healed by it, but I ask myself, "Do they need to know every detail?" So often I choose to leave out the parts that make me want to crawl under a rock or sit in the dark staring at the wall. Do I think I'm avoiding pain by not sharing the most difficult part of the journey? I was told that when you share the deepest parts of yourself, you are allowing a little light into a dark place in your soul. I want my soul to be brighter—or at least know some semblance of light.

I tried to write a book about my life that began when I was just a little girl who was molested at the tender age of five. The writing of it took me to such a dark place that I immediately had to stop writing because I started feeling unclean and disgusted at myself. Why is it that when I had no control over what was happening, I somehow felt it was my job to own the pain and carry it with me? Through the years that pain lead to me being promiscuous at an early age and resulted in me becoming a teenaged mother.

Was it really my fault that someone had violated me and, in doing so, had confused my understanding of love and affection? No, of course it wasn't. But that sense of responsibility followed me anyway. So here I stand still naked and dealing with the consequences of someone else's demons that stripped me of my innocence and opened a Pandora's box that should have been sealed for at least twenty more years.

Yes, I choose not to write that story because the emotions of rage, sorrow, pity, failure, disgust, and anger that will spill from the pages into my now settled life and because I would just like to forget all of that and move on.

So instead of allowing someone to see inside and allowing light to come in, I close it off and keep it sealed in darkness and no one gets healed—not even me! At least for now.

1. **What part of your story are you omitting?**

2. **What would happen if you allowed a little light in?**

3. **Maybe today you don't have to tell the whole story; but tell a part of it and let the light in just a little.**

A Moment to Reflect

_____

_____

_____

_____

_____

_____

_____

_____

_____

_____

_____

The Light in the Room

The harsh white light in the room was so freaking bright! I could hear all the horrors of the city happening right outside my bedroom window: the nightly soundtrack of police sirens screeching to catch criminals and ambulances coming to aid the injured. Oddly all this was "normal" in Baltimore, Maryland. It was quite a life growing up in the inner city, with all of the sights and sounds never really coming to a halt. If Vegas is the city that never sleeps, Baltimore is the city that never goes silent. There, the bars are open until two o'clock in the morning; and when they close, the party just spills into the streets and continues. Day or night you can find your friendly neighborhood dealer standing on the corner selling drugs and talking with his homies. And on the long, hot summer nights, front porches host families playing cards while listening to stereos through open windows all hours of the night. Much like the city I called home, my mind was in a constant state of chaos and noise. I never really had the opportunity to quiet my mind with so many interruptions crashing through my thoughts throughout the night—people running up and down the stairs, family members drinking and laughing, and children pretending to be asleep. But who really slept?

The light that flooded my room was one of many the city had strategically installed on street corners to deter crime. While the intention was to allow potential victims to see and avoid danger, all the light really seemed to do was keep people awake by lighting up the block and making it easier to move about. No matter how many sheets I hung to cover the window, it never got dark enough for me to fall asleep or feel safe. It's funny how some people can grow up in a place filled with so much chaos and destruction and call it normal. But I guess you just call it life in the inner city and accept it for what it is: a life where you are surrounded by poverty, crime, guns, rats, trash, and harsh lights that flood your room and prevent you from using sleep as an escape. What a terrible way to exist. But somehow, I did.

Over time the sounds of the city became just background noise that I could block out, like a television that was left on or music that I listened to while falling asleep. I always wonder: Does anyone ever really find peaceful sleep in such a place?

It wasn't until I moved to the country and literally heard nothing outside my window that I was able to grasp the concept of silence. In that silence, I heard a sound that I had never before heard in the city: nature filling the night with its own lullaby. Never had I known that there were so many beings, other than humans, communicating on this earth. In that silence I was able to eavesdrop on nature's conversations. I experienced a stillness that was deeper than any I had experienced before, and a darkness that was so complete. The darkness exposed the magnificent stars whose brilliance was brighter, and yet somehow less intrusive, than the police lights that used to flash outside my bedroom window. The stars seemed to be both near and far. The moon's soft, welcoming light soothed me, and I found rest in its glow. For the first time, I realized that the moon was what was intended to light the way at night.

I'd thought it was those damn lights that came with police sirens, ambulances, chaos, and destruction and that had separated me from myself and my sense of safety. It took me a long time to silence the city life ringing in my head and find peace and sleep, but it has been so worth it.

Living in the city had me thinking there was no peace on earth. That there was no place where someone could just sit with their thoughts undisturbed. Never could I imagine that this peace was real, and it would be found outdoors, in an environment so contradictory to my childhood, and that I would love it so fully. Wow...I guess God does have a plan and I am glad I got to this place. Just twenty short years ago, I knew nothing about silence and darkness; but now I embrace it like an old friend.

1. **What have you become accustomed to that does not serve you?**

2. **Where is your place of peace?**

3. **What will it take for you to find it?**

A Moment to Reflect

_____

_____

_____

_____

_____

_____

_____

_____

_____

_____

_____

_____

_____

_____

_____

_____

_____

Table

When I think of a table, I think about equity. Why? Because everyone can have a seat at the table.

I can remember attending dinners with my extended family as a child. The children were always told that we could not sit at the big table, and we were placed at the little table. After so many dinners at the little table, I began to understand my place and where I belonged. I, along with my cousins of the same age, became accustomed to sitting at the kiddie table without the fancy trimmings and nice silverware. At the kiddie table, we usually had a plastic tablecloth, complete with plastic forks and spoons, and paper napkins and plates.

I was never offended by sitting in my designated space. Yeah, it wasn't fancy like the big table, but it did have its perks. At the little table, we could all be ourselves. At the little table, there was no need to be proper and speak quietly. At the little table, I could talk with my cousins, be loud, laugh, and act silly. Yes, we did get yelled at from time to time for being too loud, but that was normal. As I look back at my time at the little table, I guess I never minded being at the little, less formal table because I always felt like I had a place.

As the years went by, my mindset and my needs changed. With age came more maturity and more responsibility. I began to take notice of the polished silverware and beautiful glasses and fancy plates that the big table had to offer. I yearned for a more sophisticated experience where everyone waited their turn to get food and did not push or talk over each other. It was, shall I say, a more dignified experience. Wonderful times and memories with my family were had around both tables. Our family time created the space we all needed to talk, express our feelings, catch up, listen to each other, and be heard. Whether that happened at the small table or the big table, I think we all just want to have a seat at the table.

Looking back, I think a seat where we are welcomed is what most of us are looking for in our lives. Society has established a set of rules that determine when we are to be heard, appreciated, and deemed successful. In return for meeting these standards, it promises us we will be treated equally and with respect. This ideal that we won't have to spend our time fighting and never being heard is unfortunately not always given as freely as it is deserved.

I have raised three children who have grown up to become an opera singer, a nurse, and a veterinarian. Each of them has far exceeded my expectations in establishing their own seats at "life's table." I often reminisce on how it all started out at the little table where they also had sat as children during family dinners. The little table taught them that they had a place. It taught them to not fear, but welcome transitions and promotions into new spaces. It was between these two tables that we built relationships, confidence, and opinions. It was at those tables each of us developed a voice.

1. **Have you solidified your seat at a table?**

2. **Do you remember when or where you began to develop your voice?**

3. **How do you use your seat and your voice to make the world a better place?**

A Moment to Reflect

_____

_____

_____

_____

_____

_____

_____

_____

_____

_____

_____

_____

_____

_____

_____

_____

_____

_____

Cleanse

To cleanse is to purify or wash away something.

I struggle with the idea of cleansing-—the type of cleansing that cleans my soul and allows me to impart love, acceptance, peace, and forgiveness. You know, all the stuff you read in those self-help, inspirational books—the books that claim to help you find your Zen, get your mojo back? In my effort to find my center, I tried yoga.

Yeah, for some reason I thought yoga would be great. I once saw this lady on YouTube do this awesome handstand where she lifted her entire body off the ground, rotated her legs through a few positions, and then returned to her original stance. It was amazing and motivated me to try yoga. I admired the idea that quieting her mind strengthened her body. Her inner strength allowed her to use her hands as feet and lift her body in the air. I was mesmerized by the sight of what I could only assume was some type of internal call that got her to this point. I wondered how quiet you had to be to command your body to perform such a feat. I know it probably took her years of practice and daily commitment. I could only assume she performed body-weight exercises, lifted weights, and held yoga poses for extended periods of time to get to that point. To me she was superhuman. If I could achieve such a level of mental discipline, I would be unstoppable.

So I went on a journey into yoga. I would do fifteen minutes of random yoga daily in order to gain strength and flexibility and learn to quiet my mind. The framework of yoga seemed to be focused on breathing and holding poses. As you exhale, you sink deeper into the stretch. I realized that when I focused more on the poses and not on my breathing, it always seemed harder to concentrate and hold a pose. In a few short weeks I was learning to just rest in the moment, breathe, and not let outside distractions hold me captive. I never realized how hard it was to not think about random stuff. Does my crazy mind control me, or do I control it? My instructor says it's all mind over matter and your body can do way more than you think it can.

What I learned during this process is that my mind prefers to focus on what I cannot do, instead of what I can do. It tells me I am crazy for thinking I can lose weight. It tells me I won't be able to get all this ass in the air and rotate my body. Tear my rotator cuff is what I am likely to do. LOL. Despite that mental struggle, I successfully reached my goal of doing yoga for 180 consecutive days. During those 180 days, I learned to quiet my mind quite a bit, I came to understand the importance of breathing, and I developed the strength it takes to hold my body in a steady pose. My body became limber, my core strengthened, and my mind could settle down quicker. Whenever I took a moment to do my breathing exercises, I found a sense of stillness. Though I did not reach my goal of a complete handstand with a rotation, I was extremely proud to have made it through six months of intense learning and training. What I had achieved was a great feat for me, and the physical and mental strength I gained was undeniable. I do wish I could have accomplished the handstand, but I gained much along the way. After all, for me it never seems to be the destination that makes the greatest impact; it is always the journey. Because I took the journey, I am stronger and calmer, and I found a center I didn't realize I had. I now know my body can do much more than I expect of it, and my mind is the key to it all!

1. **What journey are you willing to take to find the untapped version of yourself?**

2. **What activities can you add to your life to enhance you?**

A Moment to Reflect

_____

_____

_____

_____

_____

_____

_____

_____

_____

_____

_____

_____

_____

_____

_____

_____

_____

Solutions

Why do people constantly talk about their problems but never about the solutions?

It's funny how someone can complain about their life and never offer one solution to the many problems they claim to have. Could it be that they are just married to their problems? Is it that they want sympathy? Is it that they want you to give them an ear but not an opinion? Maybe they are just addicted to their state of mind?

Whatever the reason, it is hard to be friends with someone that continually tells you about nothing but the problems in their life. Over and over again they talk about how they don't have enough, they don't make enough, the support is not there, and their life is a mess. I am bold enough to stop and ask them, "Do you believe there are solutions to your problems? Do you think I can help you with them? Do you want my advice? Do you have a plan to change things? Or do you just want me to endure your endless hours of complaining?"

I hate pity parties, even though I do get pulled into them sometimes. I think we all fall victim to that, but we need to consider how we choose to look at our problems. I think that there is always a positive to every negative if you choose to see it. Solutions are all about what you choose to look at. Do you seek the good in things, or does the bad always seem to own your thoughts? I know that you have to train your mind to shift your perspective, but if you change your thinking, you can change your life. For example, if I have half a tank of gas, I am like, "Where can we go, man? I have half a tank of gas—let's go somewhere!" Meanwhile, other people will say, "I only have half a tank of gas, so I can't go anywhere." The facts are the same, but what state of mind would you want to live in?

I prefer to live in a happy place that allows me to live and think freely. So, for every problem I have, I commit to finding a solution before the problem even gets the opportunity to settle into a negative feeling in my heart. Having a solution in mind keeps me from continually worrying about something that's probably not worth even another minute of thought.

Motivational speaker Lisa Nichols once said, "Fear is the negative story that we tell ourselves that hasn't even happened yet." So, does it really make sense to worry about something that could be a non-issue? I remember my daughter telling me she didn't feel she had enough education and experience to apply for a nursing program. She toiled for weeks over the decision to apply. I got sick and tired of listening to her doubting herself and delaying submitting the application, so I told her to at least go ahead and apply and let them tell her no before she wasted any more time trying to predict what the outcome would be. The message for her is the same for you: Stop defeating yourself before you even start! Why would you choose to stay in a negative head space when you can move toward finding out if the thing you are worrying about is worth the energy you are giving it?

I have grown to understand that everything is an exchange of energy. What type of energy do you want to release into the universe, and what energy would you like to receive in return? I believe that what you think about, you bring about.

Take a moment to look at your life. Are you attracting positive outcomes and solutions to the many questions that flow through your head daily? Are you trying to cultivate a life full of solution-oriented thinking? Will you allow the positive energy to reside within you and constantly push out the negative talk and self-doubt that keeps you stagnant and depletes your energy? I suggest you choose love, light, and energy overall. Starting now, immediately seek solutions for the so-called problems that fill your mind. No matter what the situation, you have a choice to think about it in whatever way you would like. Which mindset will you choose?

1. **Do you tend to worry about things even before you need to?**

2. Take a moment to write down some of the problems currently occupying your thoughts.

3. Now take a moment to write down possible solutions for them.

A Moment To Reflect

_____

_____

_____

_____

_____

_____

_____

_____

_____

_____

_____

_____

_____

_____

_____

_____

Load

It was a load off my mind knowing that I was not alone in my plans for success.

Every time I tried to deviate from my plan, something (or someone) stopped me from getting off track. It seems all you need is a determined mind, focus, and a plan, and you have created an environment for success. That plan can set you up for the next opportunity that awaits you. So, what task is waiting for your obedience? Yeah, I said obedience. I believe in God and all that He has to offer me, but I know I have to be obedient to His word. Jeremiah 29:11 says that God has a plan for my life, plans to prosper me and not harm me. Plans to give me hope for the future. I love hope. I see hope as the excitement for something about to come. But sometimes I wonder, *How does hope differ from expectation?* Hope, like an expectation, sits in a space where you are anxiously awaiting something to happen that has not happened yet. I guess they are about the same thing.

I have great expectations for my life. I know that I will see my dreams manifested if I just put in the work and move toward those expectations. Heck, my motto is: If you say it enough, if you see it enough, and if you move toward it, then "it" becomes a part of who you are. So, am I speaking with power and authority over my life when I talk to myself and others? Am I taking time to visualize my future and the abilities that I have to create the life I desire? Am I moving toward being that fit entrepreneur leading and empowering hundreds of people to go out and take over the world? Success is calling me, but am I really listening?

That last question reminds of an experience I had when God spoke to me. Out of the blue, God clearly told me to give the church $453. I tried everything I could to make sense of this request, but I came up with nothing. I went to my husband and told him about it, knowing that he would say we don't have money like that to give to the church. But to my surprise, he said, "If God told you to do it, I suggest you do it." I even tried to skip church that day so I would not have to put the money in the collection plate. But ultimately, I decided to go. As the pastor began to preach, I wrote the check and sat it on the bench next to me so I wouldn't be tempted to change my mind and not place the envelope in the offering. After setting the check down, I began rifling through my Bible and saying to myself, *This does not make sense. Why $453, such an oddly specific amount?* My husband glanced over at me and whispered, "What are you doing? Listen to the pastor." As I shut my Bible and looked up, the pastor said, "Just like it says in Isaiah 45:3, God will give you the desires of your heart, 'hidden treasures, riches stored in secret places, so that you know that I am the Lord, who summons you by name."

Hearing those words unlocked something in me and I began to cry, profusely. I knew from then on, I had to do what God told me to do, and He would give me the desires of my heart if I followed His plan for my life. His lesson was not about the money, it was about obedience, trust, and His plan. It is God's plan for my life that keeps me hopeful, focused, and loaded with expectation for a grand future.

1. **Do you have an expectation for your life?**

2. **What is that expectation and whose voice are you listening to get you to that place?**

A Moment To Reflect

_____

_____

_____

_____

_____

_____

_____

_____

_____

_____

_____

_____

_____

_____

_____

_____

_____

Forgiveness

Am I in need of forgiveness? Is someone in need of my forgiveness? Though my conscious mind seemed to mark what had just happened as simply a dream, my repentant heart seemed to weep tears meant to cleanse the soul.

In my dream, I was in a house full of people. It seemed that a celebration of life for a child—my child—was happening. The loss felt deep and saddening. The people around me flocked and chattered in my face, trying to distract me from the pain I was feeling. Exhausted from the entire ordeal, I had walked into another room where I'd fallen asleep and woken up feeling empty. In this dream I was surrounded by people and yet I felt as if someone was missing.

As I jumped out of the bed to grab my phone, the very person that I needed to talk to appeared in the room. I explained to him that I was just getting ready to call him, and he said, "I am here." Somehow, I knew he meant physically and emotionally. His presence made me feel calmer. I knew that he was the one person who really knew the pain I was experiencing. He was the baby's father. We were bonded because of the life that we had brought into this world, and now we were seeing it fade away. We decided to leave the crowd and just be alone together in our grief. I felt so much better with him at my side.

Awakening from this dream, I could not help but wonder what it all meant. Hoping to find the same peace awake as I had in the dream, I picked up my phone and texted the man who'd fathered my unborn child. I told him about my dream and about the day that I'd made the decision to not have our baby. That day filled my thoughts with dark and heavy clouds. I had replayed the moment I told him I was pregnant a hundred times in my mind. His anger masked his fear, but it was anger all the same and it frightened me. I honestly didn't understand his reaction. I was a great mom, raising three kids, but none of them were his, so maybe that was the reason for his fear. The long-story-short of it was we decided to terminate the pregnancy. He was unsure about what he wanted, and I didn't want any more kids. So, I made the decision that this baby would never see the light of day, and he seemed ok with it.

How could I forgive myself for being so incredibly selfish? I knew I could have taken care of the child, but I chose not to. How did I reason myself into an agreement that this was the best decision at that time? I was so messed up— for a moment I had decided to give his baby the same last name as my other kids, because I never wanted to have more than one father for my children. God, I was so confused! It tore my heart apart making that decision.

Why was I having this dream now? What was the dream trying to tell me? How could I resolve all these feelings? Tears streamed down my face as I sat there with the phone in my hand, saying nothing to this man who had moved on so easily.

Just a few short weeks prior to my dream, he had told me about a dream that he had about me and new beginnings. As we talked about this dream, he apologized profusely for being so young and immature. He told me how he regretted allowing me to go through the abortion alone.

His apology was welcomed, but I continued to struggle with forgiving myself for choosing the quick and easy path over the hard path of love and life.

Why?

The only thing that distinguishes regrets from lessons is forgiveness. Do I deserve to be forgiven for ending a life? Does he deserve to be forgiven? Regardless of how we move forward, what I do know is this dream came to me for a reason. It was telling me that it was time to ask for forgiveness from God and this time receive it, even though I know I don't deserve it. And with that forgiveness, I pray I can find some semblance of peace in my soul.

1. Do you need to forgive yourself for something that happened in the past?

2. Healing is important to your progress, so who else do you need to forgive to move forward in your life?

A Moment To Reflect

_____

_____

_____

_____

_____

_____

_____

_____

_____

_____

_____

_____

Panda

What I love most about pandas are their eyes!

I could feel his mismatched eyes follow me as I peered over the fence to take a better look. I started thinking, *Mr. Panda, are you happy over there? Sitting there being watched by so many eyes? Being adored, feared, and loved? How does it make you feel to always be on display?*

That question rang deep inside me. Why are people okay with being mistreated for the enjoyment of others? Thinking about how we put others into uncomfortable positions reminds me of my younger days when I would go out with boys—especially the way that they would treat me. To date them was to cater to their physical needs, leaving very little air and space for myself. It was a very lonely existence, much like my friend the panda. Was he trying to figure out if this was all there was to life, like I did back then?

That panda reminded me of one of Maya Angelou's most famous works, *I Know Why the Caged Bird Sings*. I had been asked to write a poem inspired by the poet, and although I hadn't explored the book in depth, I found the title poetically profound in its own right. Why would you sing if you were in a cage? What would make you happy about that situation? Would it be because you were oblivious to the fact that you are caged? Would it be because the cage represents safety? Or would it be just because that is how you've always lived and that you've never questioned what you have been conditioned to believe? Like the caged bird, was that panda blissfully ignorant of its own captivity?

As if thinking about the caged panda wasn't perplexing enough, I also began to wonder *why* the caged bird would sing. Is it to call out to others to be released?

Is it singing a song of sorrow or joy? And, more deeply, what made my ancestors born into slavery sing while working in the cotton fields? Were their songs secret songs of hope and freedom? Could they, like the caged bird, be singing the same song? Maybe the caged bird's song was evidence of him envisioning himself flying high and soaring around the earth. Maybe the caged bird had mentally escaped the cage to travel the world. Maybe slave songs echoed their ancestors' songs of freedom still in their souls. Had the bird and the panda and my ancestors realized that while they were caged, the world could never cage their souls?

The panda, the bird, and my own experiences have made me reconsider what I've defined as my limitations. Have I caged myself with my limited thinking? Am I staying stagnant in certain jobs, relationships, and communities because of what I have been conditioned to believe? I have far more freedom than those that came before me, but I have built stronger chains to hold back my thoughts from believing in all the possibilities before me. It is more tragic to be mentally enslaved than to be physically caged. There is so much that you can accomplish with a free mind. So just as the panda sits in the zoo, and the bird is confined to the cage, I say don't allow your physical reality to destroy your true freedom. Let your hopes, dreams, and imagination burst forth and sing.

1. **What cage have you built for yourself?**

2. **What are your dreams, hopes, and aspirations?**

3. **What will it take for you to start to sing?**

A Moment To Reflect

_____

_____

_____

_____

_____

_____

_____

_____

_____

_____

_____

_____

_____

_____

_____

_____

_____

Mom

My mom's support was like no other. There are times I recall her pouring into me generations of wisdom about being a woman and forging my own path. She would tell me, "Be sure to have your own money and not let a man tell you what to do." I don't know how much wisdom were in those words because when I was married those words did not seem to sit so well with the man I married. What I did realize was that her intentions were, for the most part, coming from the right place. She had intended for me not to consider myself inferior to a man but to make a name for myself. She wanted me to hold on to my independence and not forfeit my freedom by becoming dependent on someone.

At my college graduation I remember telling Mom that I wanted to continue my studies and progress further in my education. She said, "Why don't you take a moment to appreciate this accomplishment before you dive into something else?" I asked her why she didn't want me to better my life. She said, "I understand what you want to achieve, but enjoy this moment." I was irritated by her response. I was burning with purpose and promise, and she wanted me to pull off and enjoy the view. I didn't want this view locked in me. I wanted more, and I wanted it now.

It has taken me a long time to understand what my mother was saying. She was trying to pour more of her wisdom into me by telling me it's okay to have goals and dreams, but when you accomplish something, you should take a moment to be proud. If you don't take a moment to celebrate the accomplishments along the way, you will always be reaching for happiness instead of enjoying the happiness you have at hand. I have many regrets when it comes to my relationship with my mom. She has been gone for over ten years now and I still miss her. I try not to talk about her because it hurts so badly to know she is not here with me. She is on my mind, but I only let my mind go so far down that road of remembering before retreating.

It's funny how the mind works to protect us from thoughts that would drive us into a quicksand of sadness and regret that we may not be able to readily escape. I have to keep my feelings and thoughts in check so I don't feel the full weight of the loss. And just as sadness starts to grab hold of me, I snap back and think of how funny she was, how crazy we were together, and how on one of her last days on this earth we sat in a hospital cracking jokes and laughing so hard we cried. I remember those last days so vividly, and her laughter was loud and full, just like mine. I loved hearing her laughter, so full of joy and freedom.

My mom was kind, loving, accepting, friendly, and lost at times. What I think people liked most about her was that she accepted people for who they were and did not judge them. I struggle with that daily and wish I had an ounce of what she had when it comes to accepting people. My mom was much kinder than I. We always approached things very differently. Usually I was a teller, and she was a feeler. She would ask, "Why do you feel that way?" Anyone could talk to her; she would listen and give them wisdom from her deep well.

Yeah, my mom and the struggle bus that she was is a huge part of who I am today. If I didn't have the mom that I had, I wouldn't be the woman I am, and for that I am grateful. She was a superwoman in so many ways, and all of the challenges she had to endure gave her the right to share her "wisdom" freely. And that wisdom never kept her from giving to and loving each and every one of us in her own special way.

1. **What are some important lessons you learned from your mom?**

2. **What important generational wisdom do you need to start pouring into others?**

3. **How can you show love in the wisdom you share?**

A Moment To Reflect

_____

_____

_____

_____

_____

_____

_____

_____

_____

_____

_____

_____

_____

_____

_____

_____

Still

I remained still mostly because I didn't know what to do. I had mulled over the scenario in my mind, but nothing seemed to make any sense to me. My mother always said, "If you don't know what to do, then do nothing." I'm not sure if that's good advice, and now I felt my inactivity had placed me in a compromising situation and required me to do something. It was my mindset that was keeping me stagnant.

You see, I wanted to develop this big corporation and help so many people, but the vision of what that would look like was blurry. I needed clarity, I needed focus, and most of all I needed meaning and intention. The idea of developing F.E.M.E. (Faith, Educate, Motivate, Empower) Work had become all of me and yet none of me. It was my insecurity about who I am and what I had to offer the world that kept me from gaining momentum. I felt all over the place, so my plan was to be still and know that I was headed in the right direction.

Being still does not mean being inactive. It means staying the course, not pivoting or turning, but allowing the vision to become clear while moving at a pace where things slowly but surely come into view. Maybe that's my way of not committing to anything—not allowing my mindset to change. I have to stop that negative thinking in its tracks! After all, I am moving, I am developing, and I am becoming! I lack nothing! I need nothing! I am great today and always! I am the current embodiment of all the components I need to be successful, and there are no ifs, ands, or buts about it.

Questioning myself means that I feel less than I truly am, and I refuse to feel or be less than I am! I am confident, resourceful, impressionable, vibrant, knowledgeable, positive, and loving. Why should I even question my abilities? Why don't I just embrace who I am and allow that to take me in the direction of my dreams? My God-given talents continue to open a way for me to be successful. So where is the disconnect and why is my mind so scattered? Maybe it's good versus evil playing out in my mind, like the angel sitting on one shoulder telling me I am good and the devil on my other telling me I'm really not that good? They say the one that gets fed the most becomes stronger. Am I starving the voice of encouragement and empowerment? Is the negative voice fat and happy because it gets all the attention? Wow, what a way to look at things. I am starving the most important person needed to achieve success in my life. I want that positive, affirming voice to be fed but not fat, confident but not egotistical, focused and empathetic.

Maybe I will give her some grace and try to love on her every day, not every now and then. I know she is waiting for me to get my shit together and stop allowing fear and uncertainty to keep us from being on the same page. Who wouldn't want to be their most confident self? I know I would. Listening to that better self would save me a lot of heartache and headache. I wonder: What does that confident, strong, empowered person look like? Have I ever met her? Is she perky and funny like me? I think I need to make a new friend with that voice and change my mindset. It is time!

1. **Are you questioning your talents and abilities?**

2. **If so, how can you feed your good attributes and starve the bad ones?**

3. **Take a moment to list five positive things about you.**

A Moment To Reflect

_____

_____

_____

_____

_____

_____

_____

_____

_____

_____

_____

_____

_____

_____

_____

_____

_____

_____

September

Today marks the beginning of September.

For me, September signifies beautiful beginnings and beautiful endings on so many levels. The trees begin to die off and start to change colors, offering a brilliant, magnificent array of reds, oranges, and yellows. It's funny how the fading of life of a tree can produce such beauty while the passing of a person is not so spectacular.

My mom was born on September third and she was a rare beauty. Though we, like most mothers and daughters, had our challenges, she was really a beautiful soul. She aspired to help people even though she never got the hang of helping herself. She would always try to impart wisdom to the younger generation, although in my eyes some of her wisdom was definitely questionable. I remember a time that she told my daughter that if she liked girls, it was okay, and that she should pursue that if she wanted to. I told her, "Hell, nah! And don't be telling my kid that!" Though we disagreed in principle, I appreciate that she was trying to be helpful by giving my daughter the space to figure out who she was without fear of judgment. Me, on the other hand, I was—how do you say it—judgy, judgy, judgy! (Ha! I can laugh about it now). It's funny the things you remember. My mom was always a beacon of acceptance. The kids loved to talk to her and would tell her things they wouldn't dare tell me—and I liked it that way.

Another September memory was the death of my marriage. For so long my husband and I were so happy to be married; and from all appearances, we were the perfect couple. We matched each other's drive and commitment, but we struggled with the love part. We loved each other differently and it became more apparent as the days and years progressed. I thought I could love him past his pain. I felt like my love was pure enough to cover his hate. That was such a joke!

Did you know the likelihood of changing someone is a little above zero? People have to first see a problem with themselves and then want to change. Change is a hard road for most of us because we don't want to see ourselves for who we really are. We want the beautifully painted picture that we have so carefully sculpted in our minds to be the real us. Rarely is that person based on reality, but we uphold that fake, finger-painted, pencil-drawn version of ourselves as who we really are. Sadly, the slightest problem in life splashes water all over our masterpiece, making a big mess. We soon see the image of who we wanted to be is not the truth. As hard as we try, we can no longer keep the colors clear and the lines sharp.

Like leaves changing colors on trees, the deaths of loved ones and the endings of once-great relationships are inevitable, each signifying the end of a season. All of life's situations have a process, and we have to endure all of the stages of life in order to experience the fullness and acceptance of all that life is supposed to be.

September reminds me that change is inevitable and that how we embrace that change can bring new life.

1. **What relationships have you lost?**
2. **What lessons have you learned from those relationships?**
3. **How did you bring a false image of yourself in those relationships, and how can the real you show up in future relationships?**

A Moment To Reflect

_____

_____

_____

_____

_____

_____

_____

_____

_____

_____

_____

_____

_____

_____

_____

_____

_____

_____

Failed

At first, it seemed like a failed mission.

We had made all the right choices and tried to be thorough in our planning to ensure a positive outcome, but it still felt like a failure.

For years I had dreamed of hosting a business conference with me as the keynote speaker along with other speakers that held the same vision of helping people. I wanted the attendees of this conference to walk away with so much positive energy, action items, newly discovered confidence, and direction for building and growing their business. I had spoken about business planning, how to create an actionable plan for success, and defeating naysayers so many times I could do it in my sleep.

This time, I felt I had hit all the really important points that stall small business owners. As a matter of fact, all of the speakers that spoke about positivity and having an unshakeable vision for the future crushed it! All the things I preached in my presentations were covered in this one conference. I had finally found a tribe to get the job done! Developing this tribe was no small feat. My business bestie, Anyssa, and I used the TRIBE acronym for Together Reaching and Inspiring Business Excellence. This tight-knit tribe of motivated women were standouts in their field, but until we came together hadn't known each other. Each of us were young entrepreneurs just starting in our businesses, but I knew each of us were standouts and together we were destined to make our dreams come true.

We had planned this huge event, lining up six speakers and anticipating five hundred attendees for this all-day event. Everything was meticulously planned out and we were ready to rock and roll. I even convinced my daughters to come help me as greeters at the front door. My feelings were all over the place—I could hardly believe I was finally hosting my very own conference. I could hardly stand it! Needless to say, I couldn't sleep the night before and my mind was racing a hundred miles a minute. I felt like the bags under my eyes were so heavy I would need help carrying them.

There had been so much interest leading up to the event. People said that they were coming from as far as LA to hear the lineup we had. That morning all I had on my mind was how many people we were going to inspire and help build their businesses. I was hoping to get so many clients to sign up with my company as a result of this event that I would have to hire help to meet all of their needs. This was my time, it was my moment, and I was going to experience 360-degree abundance. As my children and the speakers all started to arrive and get settled in, my anxiety heightened, and I began to panic and struggle to breathe. I was holding my chest and trying to figure out what the hell was going on. I couldn't catch my breath and I fell to the floor gasping for air.

Everyone started running toward me as I clutched my chest. My daughter, Queena, a nurse, told everyone to move out of the way. She got down on her knees, spoke to me in an extremely calm voice, and told me to breathe. Over and over she said, "Take a deep breath and calm down." I tried without success, but as I looked into her eyes, I found a peaceful place and I knew that she loved me and wanted—no, needed—me to breathe. As I tried to take deep breaths, I regained my rhythm. As I got up from the floor and headed to one of the rooms in the back, I told the group to open the doors and let the people in.

My youngest daughter, Jewell, had to do the welcome speech because my breathing was still really labored. I could hear in the back as she spoke so confidently and had the room engaged, laughing, and pondering questions all in a matter of ten minutes. The other speakers presented as planned, and then my eldest daughter, Jemeesa, took the stage to give the keynote address. She told an awesome story of her journey to be an opera singer and how her life would not have been nearly as successful if she hadn't had my support and encouragement. She said that because I had set expectations for her that at first seemed insurmountable, she had to believe what I told her about who she was and how incredibly talented she was. With only the belief she had borrowed, she stepped out and let nothing stop her. As she spoke, I saw people crying, laughing, taking notes, and planning action steps of their own. I could not believe I was watching my dream unfold right in front of my eyes.

Toward the end of the conference Queena came on stage and thanked everyone for showing up. She explained to them what happened and told them that I was a fighter just like them and I wanted nothing more but for them to succeed. So, needless to say, my daughters filled in the gap for me, but it was all done according to God's plan. The conference was an overwhelming success even though I never took the stage. I'm sure I could have pushed myself to go up there, but something inside said, "Step back and watch what you have given your daughters come into season." And just like I'd raised them to do, all of my daughters stepped up and took the stage and carried the torch. What originally felt like a failure due to my inability to take the stage turned out to be one of the biggest blessings of my life. What I had worked so hard to put into the universe paid off exponentially.

That day I found my girls had become themselves, and that my legacy and my life will continue even if I am unable to! The reality is, I had built the real tribe of powerful, world-changing women right in my own home.

1. **What did you experience that initially felt like a failure, but worked out for your good?**

2. **What type of legacy are you leaving in your children?**

A Moment To Reflect

_____

_____

_____

_____

_____

_____

_____

_____

_____

_____

_____

_____

_____

_____

_____

_____

_____

_____

Storm

One of my favorite songs is "I Told The Storm" by Gregg O'Quin. A few of my favorite lyrics are:

> I told the storm to pass

> Storm you can't last

> Go away

> I command you to move today...

> You can't drown me

> My God surrounds me

> That's what I told the storm!

I have always been fond of this song and the way it depicts the true nature of a storm. Life is full of storms! There are storms that come and go away swiftly, while other storms seem to linger and cause catastrophic damage. Some storms are gentle and persistent, and others are fierce and disruptive. Whatever the nature of the storm, storms tend to take you by surprise, sometimes knock you off balance, and teach you lessons all in the same passing.

I can recall a storm in my life that tore apart and re-weaved the fibers of my very being. Its undeniable force shifted my attitude, perspective, and understanding of myself and those who surrounded me. Within the time span of two months, I was forced to quit my job, I totaled my car, and I was abandoned by my husband that was supposed to support me through it all. The ground was disappearing beneath my feet, and my mind was thundering, "You can't keep a job, a car, or a man!" Any semblance of the invincible superhero that I once was had been washed away before my eyes. This storm made me rethink my entire existence. But somehow in the midst of it all, I recalled a scripture, "Do not lose heart over these trials and tribulations which is meant for your glory." It was then that I started to realize the thing about a storm is that it will always pass, and the sun will shine again.

Though life had dealt me what felt like a Category Five hurricane, I decided that this storm would not define me! Yes, the bills did begin to pour in like the rains of a tropical storm, but I would prevail. The heavy clouds of my grueling job search would block the sun, but I was determined to find the silver lining. The loneliness-induced sorrow would snatch joy out of my life like a violent wind breaking limbs from a tree, but I would still be standing. I understood that, while the storm could rage as aggressively as it wanted to, the real challenge would be remaining hopeful and patient while holding on.

The sun returned and embraced me like a mother's hug. God is still shining upon me brightly and I do know that there had to be a purpose for all my pain and agony. If I could step back and witness my life, I would see it being reassembled into a brighter and stronger version. My soon-to-be ex-husband agreed to assume some of the financial responsibilities, I used my savings to purchase a car, and my job called me back and offered me more sensible working conditions. As quickly as I'd been uprooted, I was again restored.

Enduring a storm is not easy. It takes one force of nature to battle another. The darkness of waiting seemed endless, and the clouds just seemed to linger overhead. As I watched the clouds move ever so slightly, there was a glimpse of sunshine in the distance that kept me hopeful and reminded me that there is purpose and promise in every storm. This moment did not define me. However, the way in which I faced my moment did!

This storm taught me that sometimes God has to separate you from people and things in order to get your attention. In this storm, I learned that I was validated by His love, mercy, and favor, and not the superficial things that could be swept away. God used this storm to reveal to me a more resilient and confident version of myself. Most importantly, I learned not to fear the storm because I know that the sun will shine again!

1. **How have your storms changed your life?**
2. **What have you learned from the storms?**

A Moment To Reflect

_____

_____

_____

_____

_____

_____

_____

_____

_____

_____

_____

_____

_____

_____

Run

Running has always been physically difficult for me. I feel like I am going full steam ahead when actually my legs are just going up and down with no real forward movement. It's particularly frustrating.

One of the best life lessons I learned was when I was struggling to run. I had a really great trainer who I was extremely fond of. She and I would work out five or six days per week. We would walk, jog, swim, and lift weights; her goal was to keep me active for about ninety minutes a day. She was the best motivator for me because when we worked out, we would talk about life, which helped keep us both on track.

Well, one day while I was running (and I use that term extremely loosely), there happened to be one other woman training with us. Every time we all got together to run, I could never seem to keep up with them. Often, they would leave me behind as they burned the road up and I would be somewhere coughing up their dust.

I recall one day when I felt especially defeated. As my trainer and the other woman raced ahead, I began to cry. I am sure you can picture it: me crying while doing this slow jog and looking like a hot mess. When they noticed me falling even further behind, my trainer did something unexpected: she turned around and ran towards me. As she approached, she noticed that I was upset and asked what was wrong as she joined my stride. "I am never going to be able to keep up with you guys," I said. She compassionately replied, "And that's okay." I felt myself beginning to slow down, sinking further into a sense of defeat when my trainer placed her hand on my back and said, "It's okay to cry—**just don't stop!**"

As I kept jogging, what she said to me really began to seep in. It's okay to be upset at things that distress you. It's okay to decide to pivot from one thing to another. It's even okay to be disappointed at what seems like a loss. But what is not okay is giving up...stopping...ceasing to move. It's funny how some things stick with you and resonate with your soul. I don't think she even realized what a profound statement she had made. And yet today, I can still recall that moment.

I am still not a good runner. I would prefer to eat glass than run, but it is a hard battle to make me give up. I may not like it and I may not do it well, but I won't give up.

It reminds me of a bracelet that I once saw. It read: "NEVER GIVE UP, NEVER GIVE IN, and NEVER LOSE FAITH." That is my goal, and, on more days than not, I run. But on the days when I feel like giving up, I visualize that moment on the road when she put her hand on my back and said, "It's okay to cry, just don't stop," and I straighten my crown, tighten my laces, and move.

1. **Where have you stopped?**

2. **What would be different if you started over and agreed to not stop?**

A Moment To Reflect

_____

_____

_____

_____

_____

_____

_____

_____

_____

_____

_____

_____

_____

_____

_____

_____

Books Never Written

Motivational speaker Les Brown once said the richest place on earth is the graveyard because there you will find the resting place of books never written, hopes and dreams never fulfilled, songs never sung, and talents never tapped into. Hearing him say that made me sad.

It makes me sad to imagine people going through their entire lives feeling like there is something more—something that's missing—and never acting on it. Imagine the disappointment of looking around and knowing that the life you're living was not meant to be your entire life. Reflecting on those words and all the unwritten stories created a million questions in my mind, questions like: Why are we given talents, but not courage to use them? Why would God give us talent and not tell us what that talent is? Why are we given gifts but not given instructions on how to use them? The more I thought about these questions, the more confused I became.

For example, when I was in high school, I had secretarial practices as my curriculum track. This track seemed fine until I reached the twelfth grade and noticed a display board full of other students in my grade and a list of colleges that they had been accepted to. I asked my teacher, "How did those students get accepted into those colleges?" She told me that they were enrolled in the college prep curriculum track, so applying to college was a part of their program. She went on to explain that I was enrolled in secretarial sciences and collegiate preparation was not a part of my curriculum. Upset about my stolen opportunity, I spoke with my advisor, who explained that my program was preparing me for the workforce and not college. *Why in the hell didn't anybody tell me about college?* I couldn't understand why no one had bothered to tell me that I had a choice in deciding my future based on my curriculum. I was devastated.

I believe everyone should have access to the information they need so that they can make an informed decision regarding their future. My not knowing about the college track cut me off from many opportunities that could have been available to me. The counselor made a decision for me that affected my life without including me. It is easy to live life in a box when people are only showing you what they want you to see. I had no vision and no mentor or teacher to help open up my possibilities. Without a clearly defined vision, every action I was taking was just a random effort with no movement towards a goal.

Purpose creates a directional force that gives life shape. I read a book called *Life at Performance Level,* by Curtis Zimmerman, that opened my eyes to the level of control I have over my life. I am the leading actress and the creative director of my story; I get to decide who I want to be my co-stars and how I mentally design my home, career, and experiences. Reading that book made me realize how much control I had over my circumstances, and it taught me the importance of taking responsibility for the decisions I was making. I started asking myself the harder questions to achieve more, questions like: Why am I letting this co-star steal my leading role? How did I create this or that circumstance with my mindset? I have shared my stage and spotlight with some people that should have been working on props or even sweeping the floor after the performance.

It seems really funny to think of life as a story that we create and recreate, but it's true! A few of the regrets I have is not creating and connecting to my own tribe, not setting personal goals for myself, and allowing trials and tribulations to distract me from pursuing my gifts. If I wrote another book, it would focus on the power of having expectations and about holding yourself accountable to making your life the greatest production imaginable. I am just grateful I won't be taking my greatest story to the grave.

1. **What would the greatest story of your life look like? Write it now.**

A Moment To Reflect

_____

_____

_____

_____

_____

_____

_____

_____

_____

_____

_____

_____

_____

_____

_____

_____

_____

_____

_____

Microwave

Today we have a microwave mentality.

We don't want to wait for anything! Everybody wants the informercial-under-sixty-seconds way of getting things done. We hate to go through a process because we hate to wait. If something is not working right off the bat, we decide it's not worth it and dump it and move on.

Is that what we expect from this world? Is that how we plan to be successful? Do we really think by not taking our time to cultivate, plan, and go through the process to attain a goal, we will achieve it?

Very seldom have I wanted something and found there was a straight line to get there. Yes, sometimes all the stars aligned, and somehow, I got to stage one quickly. What I realized is that stage one was a gift. The other stages took work, struggle, and sacrifice. But once I put something in my sights, nothing can distract me from going after it. I am just like a pit bull that bites down on a rope. Once I get a hold of it, it can't be taken away from me. I also can't move forward until I accomplish what I said I would.

Let me just say, for the record, that every obstacle that presents itself is a distraction. It doesn't even have to be a negative distraction—it could be something like family or love or even a promotion.

I find that I can be distracted easily if I am not locked in on a specific thing. If I am uncertain about my commitment, I will never get my mind to override the lazy button to be sure I stay on track. It's like there's a switch in my head that goes on and off and I don't know what causes it to flip. When my switch was on, I was able to do yoga for six months straight. When it was off, I ate myself into a baby coma and exceeded the scary number on the scale I had promised myself I would never see again. If I could find out what controls that switch, I would have my entire life figured out! What I really need to focus on is finding and controlling that on and off switch in my head that seems to activate and deactivate arbitrarily—and most times without my permission. How can I figure this out?

They say that after you do something for twenty-one days straight it becomes a habit. I will tell you that is nowhere near the truth. Six months of hard work and commitment and I couldn't get myself to do a downward dog if the dog was down and I had to pick it up. Or why can't I get this business plan finished if it is so important? I sit in front of the computer working on it night after night with no real progress, knowing that it is the key to my success, and it's still not finished. I guess maybe the more telling question is not why, but what? What makes me want to be healthy? And what is it that I fear on the other side of being skinny that stops me from progressing toward my goal? What is it about having a completed business plan that is so frightening? What doors await me that I am afraid to open?

I think that switch inside my brain might somehow be connected to fear—fear of what will come if it stays on too long. What is it about success that makes me want to stay two feet behind it? What is it about being totally healthy that makes me take ice cream and chips to bed at night? Maybe instead of trying to find a way to keep the switch on, I will work on figuring out these fears. Instead of worrying about how much time it will take to achieve my goal, I will make a solid commitment to not quit. I will commit to do things despite how I feel, and maybe, just maybe, the switch will flip back on and stay that way!

1. **What things have you not completed because they didn't happen overnight?**
2. **What fear is holding you in place?**
3. **What if you moved forward despite the fear?**

A Moment To Reflect

_____

_____

_____

_____

_____

_____

_____

_____

_____

_____

_____

_____

_____

_____

_____

_____

_____

_____

Tree

I love to watch the life cycle of a tree. Trees always seem to be uninhibited, unbothered, purposeful in their silence. Trees don't experience shame. They majestically advance through each stage of life, developing into everything that they are supposed to be, unbothered by who does or does not notice them. They stand tall and unconditionally provide shade and shelter to whomever finds a place among their outstretched arms. As the days grow short and the season change, so do those stately tresses. Slowly and effortlessly, they fill the horizon with colors to rival an Indiana summer sunset.

I love driving down the winding roads and seeing the yellow, red, and orange leaves hanging from the branches held high in the air by the giant trunks of brown. It makes me appreciate the vibrant diversity of mother nature. As winter approaches, the leaves begin to fall and paint my lawn with their amber and copper. As my grandkids and I play in the leaves, they crunch under our feet as if they are cheering us on. I love running through the piles of leaves that dot the yard.

Winter seems to test my endurance and belief that the beauty of the trees will return. Just as I am about to give up all hope, spring arrives, the trees call me outdoors with their new buds, and in a wink of an eye lush green leaves begin to form.

My trees and my faith return, and all is well with the world again. It's funny that the tree never makes a sound or moves, yet it is perfectly satisfied with the role it plays in aligning with all of the wonderfulness of this earth. I wonder why I am not as satisfied with my purpose on this earth as the tree. Why can't I learn to be as effortless as the tree as I move through life learning of love, heartache, birth, and death? Hmmmmm...I think the tree has it all figured out. I want to be a tree!

1. What part of your growth process do you struggle with?

2. How do you plan to live out your purpose despite that struggle?

A Moment To Reflect

_____

_____

_____

_____

_____

_____

_____

_____

_____

_____

_____

_____

_____

_____

Rainy Days

Who loves rainy days—really?

"Can You Stand the Rain" by New Edition is one of my favorite songs; but other than that, rainy days aren't on my list of favorite things. Rain makes me melancholy. In the rain, it seems like things are not as sharp or as bright as they usually are. No one wants their vision distorted by an ambiguous sheet of rain. I think most people spend their lives that way—unable to look past the next few steps in front of them, to see their potential.

Sometimes our current reality hinders our ability to see the world as we want it to be and as it can be. I believe anyone can manifest the world they want. All it takes is a strong mind, focus, love, and the belief in something higher than yourself. I am excellent at manifesting things. Want proof? When I wanted a home, it became my reality even when the financial picture did not look too good. When it was time to get a new car, I didn't play it safe. Nope! Instead, I focused on a new sports car. Now I drive in style and turn heads. When others said it wouldn't happen, I said, "Watch me!" I made my business my focus and succeeded.

Manifestation is not just about focusing on one thing for an extended period of time, it is about acting and moving toward it. I believe that if you see something enough (even if only in your mind), if you talk about it enough, and if you move toward it, then it becomes a part of who you are and part of your reality.

Inside of all of us is the feeling that keeps pulling you to be more. It calls to you to tap into untapped talent. But how do you convince yourself that you can do anything and have anything you put your mind to? Like the t-shirt says, just do it! Do it with your knees knocking and your teeth chattering, but do it!

When I was learning to ride a motorcycle, I was scared to death, but it was something I had a desire to learn. Then one day I reached a point where I could not spend any more time fearing what would happen if I tried. So, I made the decision to try. Every time I got on the motorcycle, I got butterflies. My hands would shake, but I would do it anyway. Despite the first few moments of the ride being completely terrifying, I loved the freedom I had aboard that powerful machine. I was loving life.

Fear stops most of us from being who we want to be and doing what we want to do. I have redefined what fear means in my life as **F**ind **E**very **A**vailable **R**esource. What does this mean? If you have a fear of riding a motorcycle, then you can access resources that prepare you to embark on this new task, such as a motorcycle safety class. The key to conquering any fear is to gain knowledge and take action. Is there something that you are scared to try? Find someone that is doing it, ask them a million questions until you feel like you have the required knowledge to do it, and then act. Will the fear and jitters immediately subside? No. But over time you will build enough confidence and courage to overcome your fear. The only way you can fail and allow fear to win is by not trying!

1. **What are you afraid of trying?**
2. **What resources do you need to pursue that thing?**
3. **Who has those resources?**
4. **How can you connect with those resources?**
5. **What action are you ready to take NOW?**

A Moment To Reflect

Questions

I have so many unanswered questions about my life—questions like: Why am I really here? Why did I have the children I have? Why was my life so rough? Why wasn't my family normal? Why were my parents drug addicts? Is this really my best life? Yeah, I have lots and lots of questions.

Most of the answers to these questions are revealed to me in different ways, but they rarely make sense. Someone once said that if you hadn't had the parents you had, then you wouldn't be the person you are. Would I change who I am? Nah, I really don't think so. But I sure wish I could have changed my parents at times. It's not that my life is glamorous, or that I have amassed great riches, it is just that I wouldn't have the spirit I have if I were someone else.

If I hadn't gone through the tough times I did, I wouldn't have become this solid person that I have become. I am so incredibly proud of how resilient, resourceful, wise, and loving I am.

My recent request is for clarity in my life, because I often wonder why I expose myself to situations that I know have a high probability of turning out to be bad. I blame that tendency on stupidity and hopefulness, which can often look the same. For example, in order to be a runner, you have to run. Your feet will ache, the shoes will cause blisters on your feet, and you will be tired, sore, achy, frustrated, and slow at times, and all for one goal: to win a race, or maybe more simply to call yourself a "runner." None of your success would be possible if you didn't first endure the pain of training.

I have to learn to view my life as training for a future race. There were times I was being trained by the school of hard knocks. I was actually born out of a love affair that was filled with deceit, lies, and betrayal. You see, I'm the result of my mother having sex with her husband's best friend. How could a beautiful beacon of light and love like me come out of such an ugly situation? Then I realized that having a different father than my sisters did not make me "special" because he was a drug addict, just like my mom. So, I didn't get the prize of being the standout exception. But I am thankful I am here, and I am grateful I didn't allow that situation to define me! When I became older and got into trouble like everyone expected me to, I realized that something felt different about who I was and what I was doing. I think it was the love I felt I was missing in my life that led me to act out in one way or another. You see, my sisters' father never really connected with me, but that was fine too. However, I did have some awesome experiences of spending time with my father's family, though he was seldom around. His family was great and gave me somewhere to feel special and have a little pride for them being "my part" of the family.

But for most of my life, belonging has been a longing I have struggled with. Trying to find out where I fit in on this earth has been a struggle. Why do I feel like I am always searching and looking for someone so unavailable to me? I guess it's because I have never settled into who I am at my core. Does that make me less whole? I think not! It just makes me alive. Every one of us has something broken inside; we just have to choose what will define us. Who will you let use that brokenness against you? And will you choose to hold onto the brokenness or will you open yourself up to the possibilities? I think we all have questions about our existence and seldom any answers. But I guess the biggest question is WHO AM I and why do I see myself the way I do? One day I see myself as the best thing since sliced bread, and the next day I can't fathom how people can bear me. I guess that is the fickleness of the mind.

These days more and more I see myself as someone that will conquer this and all other negative messages that try to break the awesome person that has emerged out of so much ugly. I AM ME—that's who I AM. Just me—with all my flaws, inconsistencies, kind heart, positive attitude, great energy, sarcastic snap back, crazy sense of humor, big hips, full lips, and a beautiful mind. Yeah, I am ME!!

1. **What are some tough things you've experienced that you have had to accept about yourself?**

2. How has that acceptance pushed you toward greatness?

3. What is your greatness?

A Moment To Reflect

_____

_____

_____

_____

_____

_____

_____

_____

_____

_____

_____

_____

_____

_____

_____

_____

Dull

My grandmother taught me to never dull my shine for anyone. She would tell me over and over, "Stand up and be who you were called to be, and stop worrying about what others are doing." Grandma always loved me but sometimes expressed disappointment over my questionable choices. I have been guilty of dulling my shine and from time to time being less than I am just to accommodate others.

Being dull and small is not a good look on anyone. Dimming your light to make room for others causes you to prioritize others' needs over your own. I wondered, *Is this the way my life will be—always following the crowd, settling for less than I am, and putting myself at the bottom of the list?*

I realized this was how I was living my life. I always took up the role that was expected of me as opposed to setting the stage for what I needed and wanted. I wish I could blame others for this, but was it really their fault? I think we pretend and put on fronts about who we are when we embark on new relationships. And when we come to an impasse, we wonder, *How the hell did I get here?* We start asking questions like, "Why am I not being valued in this relationship?" "Why is it that other people's needs are trumping mine?" The crazy part is that after it all falls apart, we always seem to reemerge.

When you stand up for yourself and allow your light to shine, some people are startled by how bright you are. Who you truly are will always find a way to surface. When you move into who you are supposed to be, others get uncomfortable, and you will hear statements like: "It never bothered you before!" "We always do it this way!" "It seems you are changing, and I don't like it." Yeah, stupid comments from people who are not prepared to experience the full essence of your presence. Had they paid closer attention, they would have seen that you are an extremely bright light and no matter how much others try to dull your shine, you are still as bright as the morning star.

When you decide to step into who you truly are, you begin to show up as the authentic, unapologetic version of yourself. When you decide to operate as who you were called to be, you begin to speak louder, walk taller, and show up for yourself and others, which ultimately makes you feel empowered.

Then suddenly you are challenged with how to handle individuals who have benefited from your dullness. You will have to choose between someone else's happiness and your own. So, what do you do? Do you stand up and try to force them to see the real you, or do you just walk away and allow the absence of your light to leave them in the darkness, which is their existence without you?

When you decide to be your authentic self you will notice that so many more opportunities will begin to open up for you. So many of us settle for much less because we are afraid of how powerful we truly are. How valuable are you to this world? How has your existence brought light to others? Do you realize that dulling your shine for one or two people can cast a shadow over other people that depend on your light?

It took some time for me to realize that it is really selfish of me to dull my shine for another. It affects the part of the world that is my responsibility, and it leaves those counting on my gifts and talents in the dark. I wish I would have realized that giving up so much of my power could alter my destiny and cause me to live outside of my purpose.

If I am being honest with myself, I was never comfortable or happy dulling my shine. We all need to begin to live authentically, step into our fullness, and accept that anyone who gets access to us must be ready to step into the spotlight. And if they are not ready, then they need to put on some shades and step aside because we have work to do—and that work requires us to shine as brightly as we can so that the people that need our light don't settle for the fake, low-voltage, dull versions of us.

1. **In what areas of your life can you be bolder and shine brighter?**

2. What positions have you been in where you felt you needed to be less than your authentic self?

A Moment To Reflect

_____

_____

_____

_____

_____

_____

_____

_____

_____

_____

_____

_____

_____

_____

_____

U mami

I describe myself as umami, a savory type of person. I have a sweet side, a sour side, a bitter side, and a salty side. All these flavors encompass who I am. Each of these sides has and continues to serve me well. Let me explain.

My sweet side allows me to engage with others and genuinely care about their well-being. My sweet side keeps me from judging people. This side is more accepting and reserved then any of my other sides. It's the biggest part of who I am. I think most people view me as sweet. It's who I am most comfortable being, so I settle in and live there often. In the sweet side, my responses are generally more positive and pleasant.

But there is also a sour side—the side that keeps people from trying to run over me. It keeps me alert to what I label as "nonsense." People who try to fast talk or get one over on me earn the privilege of seeing my sour side. Sour me is not seen on a daily basis, but she's in there! My sour side allows me to speak my mind. I feel like the sweet side gets me what I want and need most often, but the sour side is needed to level some things and some people out. The sour side's sharp tongue and quick wit keeps me grounded.

Bitter is not a term I like to use to describe myself or a state that I allow myself to remain in for long. But bitter me does rear its ugly head every now and then. When people take advantage of sweet me over and over again, it makes my bitter side appear. It's not the situation as much as it is the fact that I did not address the issue at the start that bothers me the most. I think bitter me stems from regret. Bitterness has never served me well, but it does keep me from forgetting the pitfalls that might trip me up if I turn off my BS meter. Bitterness is a kind of warning light for an alarm system that flashes red to indicate that I am about to steam up and explode.

Then, there is my salty side. I like to call her Sassy; she is my favorite. She knows she is cute! She runs around confident and free. She shows people how to treat her and accepts nothing less. She lives in a headspace absent of fear and insecurity. She holds her head up and confidently speaks on subjects she knows nothing about. I love Sassy! She is the essence of everything powerful. Confidence is her birthright. She lets nothing and no one disturb or blur the vision she holds of herself. Sassy speaks in a tone that makes people stand up and listen. When she enters a room, it gets just a little brighter because she is there.

Sassy is who I would love to be 100 percent of the time. But the truth is I love and embrace all the sides of who I am. Yeah, the sweet, sour, bitter, and sassy sides all make me a beast, and each has a purpose that serves me well. I am me and all my sides live and breathe here.

I am umami!!

1. **Are you accepting all the versions of yourself?**

2. **How do you use each of your sides to your advantage?**

3. **Which side of you would you like to embrace most of the time and why?**

4. **Which side of you would you like to see less of and why is it not serving you well?**

A Moment To Reflect

I am a Storm Coming

I am a storm coming—that's how I feel about life.

I see myself as a disruption to the psyche. When I arrive in your life, I try to pull you out of your comfort zone and lead you to a better life. That is just who I am. I want you to be and do better, to develop and live your dreams. It can be difficult to get people to see themselves as positive, prosperous, and successful. For most folks it's easier to see themselves as lazy, unworthy, and struggling. I don't fully understand why that is. Why do people tend to believe the worst about themselves instead of seeking out the best? I don't know why; but when I show up, I challenge them to see themselves as children and push them to remember what it was like to be carefree and have the whole world at their fingertips.

If I could get you to imagine you could be anything without one ounce of resistance, what would you be? What would you do? Would you choose to become a lawyer, doctor, football player, or maybe even president? When I roll in, I take inventory of all your talents that got you to where you stand. Some will say, "Skip me," because they feel they don't have any talents that could help them become all I know they could be. But this storm doesn't move on quickly. No, I will sit with you and push down on you till you find that thing inside of you. I begin to ask probing questions like: Are you capable of reading? Are you resilient? Are you hard working? Are you still standing? When they can answer back who they are and list a few of their skills and talents, then I may give them a pass.

You see, everyone has a dream inside them; but most are afraid to allow themselves to believe in that dream because they think their vision is too unrealistic. I believe my job is to come in hard and fast, to blow so hard I destroy all those defeating thoughts out of you. When this storm rolls in all deep, dark, and foreboding, you stop in your tracks and find out really quick what your priorities and strengths are. I remind you that you have a vision of your better life, and that unless you take hold of it, it's going to be lost. I rain down on you until all that stinking thinking is washed away, and in the process I remind you of the superpower you have inside. You see, like me, you are a storm coming, a dream builder, and a forecaster of a better tomorrow, and the rainbow that follows you is filled with hope.

I am a storm coming and so are you!

1. **What is your superpower?**
2. **In what ways are you equipped to disrupt old patterns and systems to develop the new you?**

A Moment To Reflect

_____

_____

_____

_____

_____

_____

_____

_____

_____

_____

_____

Freedom

It is the freedom to be me that I enjoy the most. I fought the process that I had to go through to get here, but I would say it was well worth it. I am now fifty years old. I own my own home and two cars. My children are grown and on their own, and my time is my own to own. I would have never envisioned my life to be the way that it is, but I feel free and I love it.

My newly claimed freedom is like nothing that I have ever experienced in my life. This is the first time that I have ever lived alone. Till now I have always had either a man or my children to keep me company and run my schedule. At first, being physically alone scared me; it was as if the space around me had expanded tenfold. It scared me not knowing who, if anyone, I could depend on. I have known what it was like to have my children depend on me, but for some reason, depending only on myself feels very different. It's as if I own my own life (imagine that!). If I don't like something, I don't buy it. If I don't want something, I set it free. If I don't want to do something, I don't do it. I am responsible for no one except myself, and I live every moment on my own terms.

Is this freedom? Or am I just being lazy? *Kind of!* Is my free thinking an excuse to not wash the dishes or take out the trash? Maybe! Is it a reason to dump a guy and pick up a new one if I feel like it? Why the hell not?! I have been reckless at times and I knew it, but I feel empowered. I don't have to answer to anyone for my choices. Freedom? Yeah, freedom.

I wonder if this is how most people handle this stage of their lives. Did they drink or party too much? Do they shut people out? I need to ask around. Maybe I should find a new group of people that are in the "freedom" stage of their lives. At this stage I just want to find a space for me in this world, a space where I can be my genuine self, free of others' expectations and judgments.

At times in my life I wonder: What am I doing to be productive? Do I have to be productive? Am I using my time wisely? With each passing moment, am I trying to get to know myself better and from time to time recalibrate the scales of my inner being? These questions are extremely important if I am to take advantage of the time I have been gifted to spend all by myself. Spending time alone is probably one of the most challenging things to do, but I am committed to figuring out who I am and what makes my heart sing. Today I am choosing to experience freedom in a droptop two-door convertible with my hair in the wind and my music blasting. Now let's ride out and find ourselves some more freedom!!

1. **In what areas in your life are you able to experience freedom?**

2. **If there are none, where can you create freedom for yourself?**

A Moment To Reflect

_____

_____

_____

_____

_____

_____

_____

_____

_____

_____

_____

_____

_____

_____

_____

_____

_____

_____

_____

_____

The Bird

The bird flew in as swiftly as it could through the open sliding door.

I watched in amazement as it fluttered around the room and then headed towards the window. Though it could see its natural domain, it couldn't smell the flowers or feel the warm breeze through the closed window. It was trapped. As the bird scrambled up and down the windowsill, hopping, moving swiftly back and forth, and trying to fly back into the wide-open sky, it seemed to become frustrated. I anxiously...no, nervously...*no, let's say what it was*...fearfully ran back and forth screaming about a bird in the house that needed to get out! Soon I realized that I was helping absolutely nothing. Amused by my antics, my grandson began to boast, "I'm braver than you. I can get it." Unhindered by pride or ego, I was happy to let him take a shot. Standing back, I tried to coach him as he attempted to capture the bird, but our failed attempts resulted in both of us screaming and running out the door.

After a while, it seemed the bird had found a new home on the windowsill, and I was more than willing to allow it to own that place. My beautiful, peaceful room had now become a bird cage. The bird would fly from the top of the bed, onto the windowsill, and then under the bed and back to the windowsill. At one point I had lost track of him and thought he may have flown out, but I could hear something moving and was terrified to go looking under the bed, to say the least. Why was I so scared of something so small? I wanted the bird out just as much as he wanted to be out. I only became more perplexed as the bird dove under my bed.

If you love the light, why choose to hide in the darkest part of the room? I wondered, looking at the bird. *Is that what I do? Do I go into the darkness to try and figure out how I get myself into such messes?* I thought about the mess I got into when I told myself and the gentleman I was seeing that I didn't entertain men with small children. I told him I was in a different place in my life and small children were not a part of that makeup. But then I fell in love and the elephant in the room became bigger and bigger. As his time became more and more restricted by the needs of his children, I became more and more distant. It seemed I was waiting all the time and never really getting what I needed from our relationship. I continued to stay and wait in a dark place, much like the bird.

Oh, yeah—back to the bird.

As I was hiding in the closet and calling my friend Ann to tell her that a bird had flown into my bedroom, the bird had taken flight again and ended up in the bathroom. She told me to put up a towel and push it toward the open door so the bird would fly out. Instead I took the throw off the couch and proceeded toward the bird. As I got closer, I launched the throw onto the bird and took off running in the opposite direction—straight out the door screaming. What was that going to accomplish? Now, I assumed the bird was under the throw while I was outside. *Ann comes up with the best suggestions.* After I tiptoed back into the bathroom, believing the bird was under the throw, I saw the bird sitting right beside my trap and looking at me like, *What the heck did you do that for?* I was tickled but still terrified. Ann told me to try to open a window and see if the bird would fly out. The bird flew around aimlessly, hitting the window. He really wanted out. I headed for the window on the other side of the room and began to struggle to remove the screen. It seemed to take forever, but the screen finally came loose. Meanwhile, the bird was still flailing to get out of the other window, which was closed. Instead of taking notice of the free and open space, he continued to bang and bash himself against the closed exit. That caused me to wonder: *Why is it that as people we never see the exit door that God opens for us, but insist on banging and bashing our heads on closed windows? Why is it that we become content to continue to hit our heads in the same place, pacing back and forth, praying for answers to a situation that we have already been set free from?* Well, the bird eventually heard the calls of the other birds announcing his freedom was just on the other side of the room and liberated himself.

That was one hell of an adventure for me. I hurried to put the screen back into the window and, regaining my peace, I settled back in and asked myself, *When will I take advantage of the open window that offers me an escape? What is keeping me from realizing there is another way to live instead of banging and bashing my head up against a situation that will not resolve itself?* Maybe one day I will be as smart as that bird and listen to the call and choose to turn towards that open window and find my freedom.

1. **Are you currently in a situation where you feel stuck?**

2. **What would an open window of freedom look like?**

3. **What strategy can you use to fly towards that freedom?**

A Moment To Reflect

_____

_____

_____

_____

_____

_____

_____

_____

_____

_____

_____

Amazing Day

I could feel in every bone of my body: the day I didn't know I needed and could have never anticipated. It was time to put up or shut up. It was going to be an amazing day. Let me give you some back story...

In a summer filled with fear and anger over the killings of Ahmaud Arbery, George Floyd, and countless other black people by the police, my heart was heavy. My outlook on life was bleak. Isolated and alone due to pandemic restrictions, all I had was time on my hands. The news seemed to be filled with people dying from COVID-19, the economic impact of the virus, and the toll it was taking on everyone. It seemed the world was in a state of chaos, and I was sitting in the middle of it paralyzed. I felt defeated. Even though I still had a job, and no one in my family had fallen ill with COVID-19, it didn't lessen the impact of how my heart ached for so many people.

The world was in turmoil, and I didn't know what to do. Ann, a good friend of mine, decided we should write. She said putting pen to paper to express our feelings would be a good outlet to release some of the heaviness during this time. Here comes the amazing part: Writing made me want to get up in the morning! Writing gave me a reason and a purpose. Ann doesn't know that her simple suggestion saved me during a time that I didn't know I needed to be saved. As Ann and I wrote in the mornings and shared our hearts with each other, I realized that I began to feel lighter. I wrote about anything and in any way my heart led. My stories, if I do say so myself, are awesome. Over time I went from writing short paragraphs to writing complete pages while conveying a single thought. It was great!

Late one evening, while talking with my daughter about the deaths of so many black men at the hands of police, I felt a darkness of despair descending. Unable to focus any longer, I went to bed still saddened by so many senseless deaths. The next morning, I heard the words: "Who will love our black men?" I immediately got my pad and began to write a poem. The words flowed out of me. It was as if I could sit right in the center of the souls of those black men and feel their pain. The words seem to flow like a flood of injustice, inequities, hate, and disdain, and yet I wanted to respond with compassion. I knew the poem had to be written as the words poured from my heart: "As I think of the burden the black man has had, no, continues to endure, the future of my sons, brothers, and fathers makes me feel unsure."

I didn't think I had it in me, but "Who will love the black man?" was the right message for the right time. The amazing day was not in the discovery of writing or even in the writing of the poem, but in the sharing of my message with the world. I am excited thinking that some black man will realize that black women are paying attention and that we see and love them. I was hopeful that other races would take the opportunity to put themselves in the shoes of a black man and realize the historic and systemic injustices imposed on them. On this amazing day I got to be heard! I got to tell the world my viewpoint on the treatment of black men and how they must feel existing in such a place. I got to stand up and make my three-minute contribution to the fight for justice and equality. And that in itself is amazing!

1. **How do you feel about what's going on in America today?**
2. **Instead of sitting in those feelings, let them out: Write about your hopes and dreams and disappointments regarding our country.**

A Moment To Reflect

Sleep

Sleep doesn't come easy to me some nights.

It's hard for me to get my mind to take a break and just chill out. Shutting down is a very daunting task when you are super excited or extremely worried about something. Quieting your mind is a skill that I have yet to fully develop, but I'm trying. The pictures I have seen of the Buddha statue, showing a rather large man sitting with his legs crossed and back straight and looking calm and peaceful, is my idea of being able to shut down. To me, it looks like he has transported himself into a different dimension and all that is left of him is the vessel that is his body. Inner peace and quiet can transport you to another place where blue-green waves crash against the rocks and then slowly fall back into the sea. Or maybe you are more likely to be transported to a field of green grass with yellow daisies that bloom for as far as the eye can see.

Regardless where not rushing, not moving, not making any sound, but just being calm, peaceful, and breathing takes you, the trick is to be able to get there at will. Thinking about these places do calm me. But does that mean I should be able to sit down and cross my legs and quiet my mind enough to visit those places in the recesses of my thoughts? Is that what Buddha is doing? Or is Buddha's mind running just like mine, thinking about all the things I have not done and all the work I have yet to accomplish? Maybe he's thinking about how to start a business so he can leave his dead-end job and do something with purpose? Who knows what's on the Buddha's mind and if he is truly as at peace as he seems?

Your mind can be your closest friend or your most feared enemy. It can play tricks on you and make you do and see things that are unreasonable to most. A friend's daughter has schizophrenia. She screams about invisible people touching her, and she tries to climb walls while arguing with people that are not there. Sadly, all this torment is in her mind. The same place where I am told to go and find peace is where she finds turmoil and unrest. I would love to learn to release my thoughts and sit and just be in one of those peaceful places I mentioned before. I have tried to sit with a guided meditation CD for just five minutes, and it seemed like I was there for hours. The only thing my mind could focus on was how much time I had left before I could open my eyes. Occasionally my mind would turn to questions like, "Did I turn off the stove? Did I set the alarm?" I believe the absence of thought can be a real blessing if you can train your mind to achieve it. Some level of meditation should be a part of everyone's day. With so much noise and chaos all around us, we all need to find a peaceful place to go. Maybe I will give that guided meditation another try. The reward could be extremely peaceful!

1. **What is your routine to create rest and peace?**

2. **What would it be like to find five minutes of peace in your day?**

3. **How will you start today to create your own meditation practice?**

A Moment To Reflect

Is It My Turn?

It's funny how I am always asking myself, *Is it my turn yet?*

Is it my turn yet to create something great? Is it my turn yet to be next in line to get the big blessing? Is it my turn yet for true love and happily ever after? It seems most of my life I sit around waiting for my turn. I try to convince myself that I am ready to go to the next thing or even the next level, but am I being real with myself?

I remember a time when I was listening to this lady on Facebook asking God, "When is my turn? And is there any chance You could hurry it up?" Does she, like me, wonder just how many people were in front of her? I found the video to be hilarious because of the level of anxiety she was showing towards God. But how many times have we asked the same questions? If you're like me, you probably feel like you have put in all the work and waited, but to no avail. You are in the same spot, asking, "Is it my turn yet?" too. I personally think that progress is often slow, almost invisible, and you don't even realize you are moving forward. Wouldn't it be awesome if we could be SOOO focused on the goal that the work to get there did not even seem to be a problem? I like that idea.

I want to become the type of person that can't be distracted no matter what. Am I that person today? Hell, nah! Can I be that person? Maybe. In many ways, I feel in some areas of my life my switch is on and focus and determination are mine. But most often the switch shuts off without warning and I can't even find the switch to turn that bastard back on. Regardless, why does it take such a long time to be successful?

I wish I could answer that question. But what I have learned is it all depends on what success means to you. Is it buying a car? Then success can be fairly quick—if you have the down payment and halfway decent credit, then you can get pre-approved instantly. But if the goal is the pay cash for the car and walk off the lot owning it outright, it may take longer. The work of saving that type of money can take some time, but owning a vehicle outright requires one of the most important disciplines you can develop: delayed gratification. No one wants to wait for the reward. Waiting is a bad word for most people, including myself. After all, who wants to wait to buy those shoes if you can just charge them? Get it now, worry about the cost later is where we have gotten to in this world these days.

We somehow now have a get-it-now mentality about everything. I admit I am one of those people too, but I have a daughter that has been down with delayed gratification her entire life. She will happily wait for something, save, and focus in order to achieve her goal. I remember one Christmas day when she was little, she received a lot of gifts from Santa and, like all kids her age, she was extremely excited. The difference was that she would open one gift and play with it the entire day, then open a second gift. Her sisters would push and push her to open her other gifts, and she would say, "No, they're mine, and I'll get to them later." Then a few days later she would come back and ask if she could open another gift. I would say, "Of course you can." That girl had gifts to open for over a week, and she never worried about what the next gift was until she got tired of playing with the one she had. Today, she has chosen to pay off her student loans in three years, so she is living on a tight budget and tripling her payments. When her sisters push her and ask why she doesn't want a new car or a nice house, she tells them that she does want those things someday; but for now she doesn't want to be a slave to her student loans so she's going to pay them off first. I can't even fathom having that much self-control. I would have bought me a new car and a beautiful house and all the shoes I wanted and just learned to live with the student loans. Doing it her way makes so much sense. After all, she cuts out all the extra interest on her loans and she still has a nice place to live.

I wish I had whatever it is that she has, because the girl is winning—and I like to win! Not wait, but win. And as I have matured, I've stopped asking, "Is it my turn yet?" knowing that with patience, planning, and focus, my turn will inevitably arrive!

1. What would you like to have held off on before moving forward in your life?

2. Is there something that you could delay getting today that would benefit you later when you are more prepared?

3. What is that thing and how will you use your waiting time wisely?

A Moment To Reflect

_____

_____

_____

_____

_____

_____

_____

_____

_____

_____

_____

_____

_____

Living Is...

Living is freeing. When I say living, I'm talking about embodying an internal freedom to be and do what your heart desires. Living is a state of mind.

Many people hold themselves captive by their thoughts and that is why they never seem to enjoy life. I am guilty of this myself. For example, I always say I want to travel but I never book a ticket. Traveling is all I really want to do, but still I have not been anywhere out of the country even though I have had my passport for over a year. Why am I afraid to travel? Before now no one could have stopped me from accomplishing anything I put my mind to. So why does my passport remain unused?

Living for me is exploring the colors, the shapes, and the sounds of this wonderful world.

I used to love coming home from a long day's work and just sitting around. Now, sitting around seems to be all that I do, and it has become mundane and a routine, comfortable trap. I wonder if this is what happens to relationships? Do you get so used to people that they become stale and predictable? Do you become accustomed to what the other person looks like, talks like, and feels like, and instead of appreciating their essence, you begin to be comfortable with the fact that they will always be there? Routines are often the opposite of living adventurously. I don't want my life to be full of routines and void of exploration into the different parts of this life.

I could say COVID-19 kept me from living, but that would just be another excuse, much like any of the other excuses I had prior to the global pandemic—excuses like "I have to work," "I don't have the money," or "I could use that money to fix the house." The thing about excuses is that on the surface they all seem valid, but they are still excuses.

I want to live! I want to see the world! I want to travel and explore...but. Yeah, but!! That simple three-letter word keeps me trapped. Why is "but" even in the English language? I was told that when you give an apology to someone and you use the world "but," everything said before that word becomes obsolete and meaningless. So why use it? I want nothing more than to travel, but what about the kids? I want to see the lights of Paris at nightfall, but what about the cost? I want to sit on a beach in Cabo and drink margaritas all day, but what will people say?

The real question is not "Why won't I travel?" The real question is "What is really holding me back?" What am I accomplishing by allowing that three-letter word to control my life? Living is supposed to be freeing. I need to set my mind, body, spirit, and wallet free so that "but" will no longer keep me from moving about the world!!

1. **What "but" is keeping you from experiencing new things and living the life you desire?**

2. **And what needs to happen for you to live life fully and freely?**

A Moment To Reflect

_____

_____

_____

_____

_____

_____

_____

_____

_____

_____

_____

_____

_____

_____

_____

_____

_____

Mirror

It was the mirror that gave me away.

It seemed no matter how far I walked away from it, it followed me, convicted me, and kept me from being happy. My reflection, my guilt, and my reality were all in that mirror, and for some reason I had tons of mirrors around me. There seemed to be one of these freaking things in every room taunting me, laughing at me, scaring me, telling me who I was, and reminding me of where I had come from. I hated them all. So, I began to quietly and secretly remove them from my life. Every day for three weeks I either blacked out a mirror, hid it, covered it, or took it down from the wall and placed it in the closet or under the bed.

The funny thing was that even though the spot was empty, I still somehow caught a glimpse of my reflection as I passed where a mirror had once been. Was it the mirrors I needed to deal with, or the feelings that lurked inside of me? I was suffering from imposter syndrome and guilt for leaving the hood where I grew up. That feeling that someone was going to find out that I was just "playing smart" when I'm not really smart. That feeling that somehow all my worldly possessions would be stripped of me once people realized I was just an ordinary woman pretending to be something extraordinary. It was almost like someone else had taken over my life and I was just admiring their success from the outside.

These feelings stemmed from the fact that none of my siblings made it out. They became trapped by their own thinking. They let their limiting beliefs keep them in the old neighborhood on the same block trapped in the same cycle like all those before them.

I had spent my life teaching people how to avoid getting confined by their own thoughts and how to chase after a better life. How is it that you can convince total strangers that they can be great, but you can't convince your own family that they are worthy of greatness?

Getting out was hard for me, but I decided to move to another state, buy a big house, and live the life that was calling me despite the voices in my family telling me it wouldn't work. I had decided to refuse to allow my past to determine what my future would look like, but these damn mirrors kept showing me that poor little struggling girl that wanted to be successful but had no idea what success looked like or where it could be found. It was like that little girl lived inside me and only showed up as I passed those mirrors. And when she got the chance, she would say things like, "Why do you deserve to live in this big house while your family live in the hood?" "Why do you need to vacation every year?" "Why do you have three cars in the garage when you can only drive one?" She was good at scolding me and would never get caught saying she is proud of me or that she can see how hard I am working. That little girl living inside of me never acknowledged that I had sacrificed a great part of my life struggling to get us both out of the ghetto and gain our freedom. All I could see in those mirrors was that little girl.

That little girl inside me irritated the hell out of me. I didn't know how to shake her until one day, when I decided to stop hiding from the mirrors. I pulled them out from under the bed and out of the closet. I put them where I could clearly see them. Then I sat down in front the largest of those mirrors and told that little girl I loved her. I loved her courage. I loved her determination. I loved her hard work and her big dreams. I thanked her for all she had done to get us into a better, safer, happier life. I told her that without her nothing we have now would have been possible. I poured love and gratitude into that little girl in the mirror until tears flooded both our faces.

Healing is a process that no one wants to walk through, but it is necessary. She didn't want me to forget her now that I was all grown up and successful.

She wanted me to remember she had been there when all those scars were still fresh, and it was she that held me through the pain, and she would again if I ever needed her to.

I assured her that all the experiences and traumas she endured allowed me to be at the level I am today. See, once she figured out I was not trying to leave, forget, or abandon her, she began to accept OUR success. I never could have gotten to this point if I'd continued to run from my past and leave her behind. We became one and that was the best solution for us both. Healing is a wonderful thing when you sit down and have hard conversations with yourself and decide to move forward. Today I love looking in those mirrors where I can see my past, my present, and my future self, and all of them are amazingly perfect together.

1. Who are you hiding from?
2. What would be the worst thing that could happen if you spent time with your past, present and future self?
3. What would it take for you to love the person you see in the mirror?

A Moment To Reflect

_____

_____

_____

_____

_____

_____

_____

_____

_____

_____

_____

_____

_____

_____

_____

_____

_____

_____

I Wish

I wish I was a bird.

I wish I had wings that spanned a field of freshly cut green grass dripping with dew drops sparkling in the morning sun.

Far above these fields I can see the deep green richness which reminds me of the color of money. (I wish I had money, as plentiful as the blades of grass in the field.)

Soaring low to the ground my wings touch the dew-dampened ground. The cool, damp air settles throughout my body and revives my senses. I see my reflection in a puddle that has formed, and I pause my flight to quench my thirst. The clean, fresh rainwater satisfies. The sun now shines brightly, awakening the world and all that call this land home.

I see colors, so bright and shockingly beautiful, as I ascend towards the sky. The oranges catch my eye because I love orange! I love its texture and the essence of its tones. I love the way it glows across my feathers. The many tones and hues of orange are really dynamic with tints of red, which reminds me of fire. (I am a ball of fire and very sassy.) Bathed in my glowing orange feathers I assume the identity of a phoenix rising, filled with bold, blazing confidence as I climb higher and higher into the sky.

I dive again so the world below can take notice of my beauty, my energy, my uniqueness, my inability to blend. If I was a bird, I'd be the bold orange bird that stands out as I flew over fields. I would dive into puddles unafraid and admire my shadow in the water as I darted past. What does it take to be that bold, free, lively creature that demands space, attracts energy, and exudes confidence? If only I could be a bird long enough to know.

No, on second thought, I don't want to be a bird. I wish I were a butterfly—that's it! I don't really want to go through the caterpillar phase. Who wants to crawl on the ground getting dirty and have to stay in a really dark place hoping to survive long enough to become a beautiful butterfly?

But that's the process. I don't want to do process; I want to be beautiful. Isn't that true for most of us? We never want to go through the bad to get to the good. We just want the fun part. We want the flying, the beauty, and the freedom, but are we willing to do what's necessary to earn our wings? Truth be told, no one really wants to earn their wings, they just want to spread their wings and fly.

1. **What do you dream of being?**
2. **What characteristics appeal to you the most?**
3. **Are you willing to endure the process to become the best version of yourself?**
4. **If so, what does that look and feel like?**

A Moment To Reflect

Basket

All I had to teach the class with was a basket of ideas.

I had written down a bunch of words and phrases for the students to talk about during class. It would be up to them to tell a story based on their perspective and/or life experiences. It was going to be extremely interactive and a lot of fun. It would definitely take people out of their comfort zone. I questioned if these students were ready for all I was asking of them. I knew I was ready to do something new, but were they? By making the students aware of their thought patterns, these exercises would shift their thinking and help them figure out new ways of looking at their life and other people. Getting them to open up was going to be challenging, but having worked with this group for a while I believed they were ready.

At the start of class I came into the room with my basket filled to the brim and took a seat at the front table. I had considered a couple of different ways to run the class. My first idea was to get them all to pick out an item from the basket and then take a seat. But if I did that, they would be focused on preparing their responses and not on the person speaking. So I decided to have each student pull out a question and have them speak on it immediately.

Linda was the first participant. She was a middle-of-the road type person— you know, the type who will talk if you prod them but doesn't really like the attention—because I didn't want the most talkative participant to be first and make it look too easy. Linda picked "It felt amazing when" from the basket. She was given five minutes to tell a short story based on the phrase and then the group would ask her questions based on her share. Linda stood up and said, "It felt amazing when I walked into the classroom fully prepared to ace my exam. I loved being prepared to do my best." What a great start to the class! I was super impressed. I told Linda that she did a great job explaining to us how amazing being prepared felt. I then opened the floor for the class to ask questions or give comments about her story. One student spoke up and said, "I have felt that way too, so I understand what you were feeling. Did someone make you study, or did you do it on your own?" Linda explained that she had studied on her own because she had failed the test before and didn't feel good about it. I took Linda's response as an opportunity to mention that sometimes failure can be a motivator to make you try harder the next time. I then told everyone to write that down, "Failure can be a great motivator to do better."

Tim was next to draw a question. He selected the word "Embarrassed." He took a moment to compose his thoughts and then began, "I was embarrassed when I didn't realize that I had tissue on my shoe. Thankfully, my friend pointed it out to me and then stepped on it for me!" When I asked for questions or comments, another student mentioned he'd had a similar experience but wasn't lucky enough to have someone save them from being laughed at. I paused for a moment and had the group write down "Real friends help, not hurt." We continued drawing ideas from the basket and telling stories.

This was the most rewarding class I'd had in a long time. When class concluded that day, we had eighteen great statements of positive ways to think about things. Each statement taught us about how important perspective is as well as the importance of finding the good in people and situations. This was time well spent, and the students left the class laughing and talking with a clipboard full of notes and positive statements. I would call that a success!

I think the most important takeaway was that life is all about perspective. The students learned that, if they can put things that happen to them into perspective, they can better control how they feel about those experiences. It was truly an amazing day. Leading a class like this was very rewarding. Realizing the impact I had on each person that day fired me up and made me feel I had superpowers that could change the world.

1. **What type of impact are you making on others?**

2. **What superpower do you embody that you are not currently using?**

3. **How can you use it?**

A Moment To Reflect

It's All in a Day's Work

I never realized the strides I was making toward my goals but—it's all in a day's work!

I was so preoccupied with volunteering, speaking, writing, organizing, scheduling, interviewing, and moving, that I never noticed the finish line was getting closer. It was a bit like running a race. I had an idea of where I wanted to go *(ready…)*, I put my head down and stayed focused *(set…)*, and then took off, putting one foot in front of the next *(go!)*. I moved forward one calculated step at a time. Taking each step as it came, I constantly asked myself, *Should I interact with this person or network with that person? Is what I'm doing going to appeal to the masses? How do I stay relevant? How do I make it exciting? How do I communicate my vision to others?* Moving toward my goals was not a sprint but a marathon.

Like all things of value, my journey did not come without risks. I was constantly asking myself, *What if I have a misstep or completely trip and fall?* Ultimately, the potential reward of living my purpose outweighed the risks, so I rolled up my sleeves and got to work. Not wanting to break my stride, I put myself out there. I talked to people I may have never considered approaching and was pleased that most of my steps were fruitful. Even if the conversation didn't result in a new business relationship, the opportunity to practice my pitch was worth the interaction.

"Hello, my name is Trina, and I love to encourage women to be the best version of themselves. As a result of my services, your clients will become more confident and knowledgeable about the interview process and how to navigate through the unwritten rules when seeking employment." I had gotten so good at this pitch that I could always find a way to bring up F.E.M.E. Work in any conversation. *Fewer words and more passion* was what I often told myself.

One day, while in a room full of students, I courageously told them my most compelling story, "Do Not Sit." I could tell they were hanging onto every word, taking inventory of all the words, pain, and inspiration the story held. As I closed out the final sentence and the applause faded, I heard a small voice from the back of the room. It said, "How do you muster up so much courage to tell such a story?" I explained that every time I share my experience, it turns my pain into someone else's hope. She replied, "I want hope. Hope is something I haven't had in a long time." Giving her my card, I assured her that I could help her to see hope where she now sees hopelessness. She followed up with me and we worked on her resume, interviewing techniques, and presentation. The girl was awesome. Though she was very soft-spoken, she had that little something that made me feel like she was going to do something big.

And I was not wrong. After scheduling and completing a round of interviews, she happily met with me to tell me how it went. She told me how she was prepared for every question they threw at her because she remembered what I'd said: "They can't ask you anything that you don't know about yourself. Speak up, be assertive, be confident." It warmed my heart when she told me that my voice was in her head the entire time and she felt like I was right there rooting for her. Several days later she called and told me that she received two job offers and she was so thankful for the time I'd spent preparing her for success. I told her, "It's all in a day's work!" Humbly and compassionately, she replied, "That is not true. The pain, passion, and love that you express is not a day's work. It is in the fabric of who you are." I beamed with joy and hung up the phone thinking, *Today was a good day as I stayed on track, never breaking my stride!*

1. **Make a practical to-do list specifically for accomplishing your goals.**
2. **Think about the impact you could have on people; what advice would you give them to keep them moving toward their goals?**

A Moment To Reflect

Time to Kill

My dream has always been a mission statement of defining and refining who I am. I want to fully understand where I am going in life and to discover the very essence of my being. I want my time here on earth to be spent fulfilling the dreams that revitalize and energize me.

However, lately, I have found myself having a lot of time to kill.

I never gave much thought to this phrase "time to kill."

Having time to kill could be defined as having nothing else to do, or it could be a justification for doing nothing at all. However, in this case I had been deceiving myself. I had allowed my downtime to keep me sedentary and stop me from moving forward. This time-killing was not a pit stop, it was a conscious and active decision to stop moving completely. I realized that in this case killing time was not only an excuse to not use my time wisely, but it had also become the root cause of a cycle of accepting mediocrity and procrastination as my norm.

To kill means to cause the death of something. Do you want to be the reason your dream is dying? Killing time is not an exception to the rule, and each time you choose to kill time, you're guilty of inflicting a fatal blow to your dream. I challenge you to take time to think about how many times you have found yourself to be in a continuous loop of procrastination. How does that sit with your soul? Have you muffled the calls of your purpose as you remained stuck in the time-killing zone?

The good news is that it is never too late to make a different decision and step back into action. Killing time is easy, but are you willing to do what's hard to keep your dream alive?

Each day you get the choice to remain in or step out of your time-killing zone. You get to choose to stop contributing to the death of your time, dream, and purpose, and instead decide to fight for what you want. I challenge you to not waste the time in between where you are and your destination. Start today to become active and mindful during your journey and decide to never "KILL TIME" again!!

1. **How has procrastination shown up in your life?**

2. **What effect has it had on your dreams?**

3. **What strategies can you put in place to stay focused and moving forward?**

A Moment To Reflect

Timing is Everything

Timing is everything I reminded myself as I prepared to go on stage.

I had been waiting for this moment for so long. I think I had dreamt of being on this stage for a lifetime. Today was finally the day, and I was about to inspire thousands with my words. I wanted to pinch myself because it was hard for me to believe I was about to witness my dream manifested. Or was this moment just dumb luck? I'd completed all the steps, learned the lessons, read all the books, and put my dreams in front of me. I'd made vision boards, spoken daily about goals, recited affirmations, and practiced, practiced, practiced. I'd done all the background work required to make my dreams a reality and it was tiresome, but here I was, about to step onto the stage and into my dream.

Manifesting your dream requires a constant commitment of keeping promises to yourself that you have not shared with anyone. Keeping your promises and goals a secret is the easy thing to do because if you give up, no one is the wiser. However, actually following through on promises to yourself builds self-confidence. I have found that it takes an abundance of confidence to stand in front of a group of people and be vulnerable, to open up to them and tell them stories about your life and how you became who you are. Public speaking is one of the greatest fears held by the majority of people in the world, and here I was about to do it in front of a room full of strangers. Having so many eyes staring back at you while you are trying to explain your brokenness and your triumphs is nerve-wracking.

Trying to convince them that an ordinary person can do an extraordinary thing felt impossible. But I was determined to make them believe! I could feel my hands sweating. I wish I had practiced one more time, which would have made it my hundred thousandth time. I guess no matter how many times you practice, imposter syndrome shows up—right as you're about to step into the spotlight. It's like as soon as I hear my introduction start, my mind asks, *Who are you that people should listen to you? Everybody has problems—you are not special. What makes your story different than others?* As the self-doubt screamed in my ear, I drowned out those negative thoughts with affirmations of who I am and what my purpose is. I remind myself that if only one person gets the message of hope, then I have done my job.

The time to make my entrance was quickly approaching. In my mind, I began practicing what I was going to say, but it all sounded like mumbo jumbo in my head. I'd felt so much conviction during practice the night before, but that morning I felt average. I felt like an imposter and that I wasn't the right person to do this. As fear took over, I turned to walk toward the stairs to exit the building. But as I was about to leave, I caught a glimpse of myself in the mirror. I stopped, turned, and said, "Get your ass back in there—you have earned this moment. It was not handed to you, and you did not steal it from anybody. It is your time!" *Yeah…this is my time!!* I had gone through life's rollercoasters of ups and downs and finally I was going to share how I'd overcome it all. I had earned my stripes. I am not an imposter. I am ME!

I returned to my rightful place at stage left and, as the introduction ended, I smiled. *Boy, am I blessed.* I thought. *I am really going to do this. I am really going to tell my story to an audience of three thousand people!* And with my confidence in check, I strode out onto the stage, holding my head high, strutting my stuff in my red dress and heels realizing that **timing is everything**!

1. **Have you put in the work to take advantage of the opportunities that come your way?**

2. **Are you prepared for greatness?**

3. **If not, what do you need to begin doing to prepare yourself?**

A Moment To Reflect

_____

_____

_____

_____

_____

_____

_____

_____

_____

_____

_____

_____

_____

_____

_____

_____

_____

_____

Rich

I love rich.

I love rich men.

I love rich experiences.

I love rich coffee.

The boldness of rich coffee tantalizes my palate and washes away the sluggishness of morning. It allows me to speak up, move faster, and take charge. Yeah—that little, dark, rich cup of coffee goodness changes everything.

The same can be said for a rich man. A rich man emboldens me to go out and be the better version of myself. With his kind, loving, and supportive nature, I move faster towards my goals. He awakens the things inside of me that only a man of integrity, passion, and dominance can pull out of me. I can live a vigorous and vibrant life full of color and wonder on the strength of the words that he speaks into me. He stands beside me not to compete but to complete my dreams. But it's not a rich man that does these things, it's a good man that does these things.

My kind of man is just like a good, bold, rich cup of coffee. After all, who would desire a weak, watered-down cup of joe, void of flavor and color? My coffee is black and smells strong even before it is brewed. Its strength is unbothered by the addition of water. It welcomes it, but it doesn't allow it to overtake its powerfulness. In retrospect, a good, bold man doesn't yield to obstacles that come his way. He stands firm in his beliefs, and the world must rotate around him. He does not fold to challenges. He is powerful in his own right. The strength of his convictions is unwavering and admirable.

There are so many attributes I like in a man that resembles the coffee I like. But I also enjoy cream in my coffee. It sweetens the beverage just enough to make the coffee even more enjoyable. The cream is welcomed by the coffee and gingerly submerges itself into the cup in a unified way to heighten the essence of its flavor. I appreciate a man who welcomes the warmth of a woman and values what she adds to his life. He is good just as he is, but his woman sweetens and mellows out his boldness. He embraces the lighthearted way she breaks down his rough exterior and adds dimension to who he is as a man.

Both a rich man and a rich cup of coffee have the ability to change your mood and make you perk up as you take a big whiff of their essence. I pray that your man is as bold, strong, and rich as your next cup of coffee!!

1. **Who is the person that shows up boldly in your life?**

2. **How does their presence empower you?**

3. **What in others makes you your best self?**

A Moment To Reflect

_____

_____

_____

_____

_____

_____

_____

_____

_____

_____

_____

_____

_____

_____

_____

_____

My Love

My love for myself is amazing! It's the type of love that allows me to dance when no one is watching, no matter how I look doing it. My love accepts me as I walk pass the mirror at thirty pounds overweight and tells me, "Baby, live your best life." My love sees no flaws in my actions as a woman and a free being on this earth. My love for myself is teaching me that self-love is the only real love that counts. My love is the foundation that I build upon to learn to love others. I am so blessed to be at this point in my life, when the opinions of others no longer have the sting of defeat. This morning I chose to dance! I stood up in the middle of my living room floor and I danced to "My Love" by Johnny Gill. This dance was different—it wasn't me feeling love for some man. Today I felt like the song was an acknowledgment of a change that is coming. That change of learning that my love for myself could override all others' opinions, rejections, fears, losses, and disappointments. My love will support and hold me like a bear hug when I am alone and calling out for connection. My love will sustain and keep me in a mindset that allows me to be free and uninhibited.

Oh, this dance felt different. It called up a level of love for myself that I had never experienced. It made me smile from the inside out, and it felt amazing!! I will say no to lesser love. I will be authentic in my love. I will love without abandon. I will be true to myself, and I will love who I am no matter what state I am in. I am learning more and more each day that I AM ENOUGH! I have not always felt that way, but today I felt her. I felt the presence of the woman I am called to be, the essence of who she is and the knowing that she needed me to show up. Her life and future depend on it. I need to commit to finding her absent of anyone else. I need to keep her around because she was, no *is*, so freaking awesome. You don't understand how she danced as if she was the only being on this earth, and she was more than capable of loving every inch of herself.

I am crying right now because I don't want her to disappear. I need to find a way to keep her with me at all times. How? How? You don't understand how it felt just for those moments dancing with myself and for myself. Connecting with my soul. Feeling complete. That NEVER HAPPENS! I am always trying to visualize someone else when I am alone; but today, just today, it was all me in the room, and that was all I needed.

Please, God, help me to accept, love, and invite her back into my life daily. I need what empowers her to be so awesome and to know why she felt so amazing. I know I must have looked a crazy mess dancing, but why didn't I care? In that moment I was WHOLE and that wholeness encompassed all of me. Self-acceptance, love, joy, and peace for myself is on the horizon. I feel it and will call on it daily as part of my affirmations. I know that if you say it enough, if you see it enough, and if you move toward it, it becomes a part of who you are. So today, I call on Me. I acknowledge Me. And I take the journey to self-love alone.

1. **Do you love yourself?**
2. **How can you commit to loving yourself more?**
3. **What could you do as an expression of that self-love?**
4. **In what ways do you feel self-love would make life more enjoyable for you?**

A Moment To Reflect

Oyster Sauce

What the heck is oyster sauce? Does anyone really know?

I love seafood, but oysters are not my thang, and I don't think I would add sauce to something I already don't like. Now blue crabs are another thing. I love them. When I lived in Baltimore, I used to spend crazy amounts of money on blue crabs and did it happily. I would pay over $100 for just a dozen of them. Who knows what made me think that was a great idea? What's even crazier is I would spend a $110 for just a dozen blue crabs that would only last an hour but refused to spend $60 on a class that would give me knowledge for the rest of my life.

People spend their money on what they want faster than they would spend money on what they need. For many years I had a skewed way of thinking, then one day I heard something that changed my perspective forever. During a conference in California, one of my favorite motivational speakers, Eric Thomas, said that knowing what to do was not the problem, the problem was a poverty mindset. Did I have a poverty mindset? When I think about some of the decisions I've made around money, it is totally possible. For example, I would spend my money on a Coach bag instead of a business coach, while running around talking about what I couldn't afford. What you have been conditioned to believe about money dictates your spending habits. I spent money on things I felt were important to me. But at what cost? My problem was not limited resources, it was the need to fit in while experiencing instant gratification. We all have our idea of happiness and what brings us joy, but what are we willing to sacrifice to get it? I changed my thinking and ultimately changed my life. I began to develop a willingness to invest in myself, a commitment to build my own business, and a desire to gain my own wealth.

I knew that, in order to keep my dreams in focus, I had to deal with my primary barrier to success: fear of the unknown. I realized that, since I had no vision of success and no mentor to show me what success looked like, fear kept me crippled. If I had just taken action on some of my ideas, I would have developed my own roadmap for success. I was always asking questions like, "Where do I start, what should I do next, and who is going to help me?" However, the truth is that, like most things in my life, I was the answer to all the questions in my mind. While I was assisting others and pushing them to move beyond their limiting beliefs, personally I was filled with my own fears and insecurities.

My most recent excuse for not pursuing my goals was the coronavirus, which is a valid reason. But if it was not the coronavirus it would be my financial situation, my desire to have a mentor, or my lack of knowledge. Yeah, I could reason the hell out of a way not to do something—it's a well-developed skill that has never served me well.

I have made some great decisions in my life when I moved and told fear not to follow me. When I allowed myself to show up at events or speaking engagements, even with butterflies in my stomach, big things happened. I was uncomfortable, but I never allowed those butterflies to deter me from getting things done. I am a mover and a shaker; I just can't get myself to move or shake when it comes to making time for me and my dreams. How depressing is that? So I ask myself, "What's next?" What must I do to decide to no longer sit still but instead make a calculated, decisive move toward something I want?

After telling fear to get behind me, my next step was to write down my goals and list the steps to get there. Then I developed a single-minded view of things on that list and let nothing distract me from my destination. I have been through this process a thousand times before and have always reached my goal, but for some reason I'm stuck on this particular topic. My mind keeps holding onto these limiting beliefs about where I have come from and why I can't achieve wealth. I think I did my part to instill a strong sense of self in my kids, and they will be able to take it to the next level; but hell, why can't I take it to the next level too? What's wrong with me continuing to be the trailblazer in my family, breaking the generational curse of poverty and a lack mindset? Why don't I believe that I can be the person who makes the first million dollars in my family? I can—I know I can—if only I could get my mind to believe it. Convincing others of their greatness has never been the problem for me; but an inability to recognize my own greatness has led me to stand still. As I continue to tell others, "Do not sit," where is the breakdown for me? How do I rectify this? And what has not addressing my thinking cost me over my lifetime? The answers reside in my ability to conquer my fears, free my mind, step out of my comfort zone, and try new things. Maybe I should begin by trying oyster sauce!

1. **When was the last time you tried something new?**
2. **What limiting beliefs are holding you back from living your best life?**
3. **List three limiting beliefs that you will break past in the next month.**

A Moment To Reflect

_____

_____

_____

_____

_____

_____

_____

_____

_____

_____

The Sort of Place Where...

It's the sort of place where you can put up your feet, lay down your worries, and experience tranquility, comfort, and peace.

Where is that place for me?

Over the years, I can say that I have had a complicated relationship with peace and comfort. When I was little, I dreamt of a place I could escape to that was wide open and filled with peace. In my special place, everyone was prosperous and happy and had families complete with love and support. My dream world was a beautiful place that never seemed to become my reality. Yet, I never stopped dreaming.

When I was blessed with a family of my own, the dream of that special place I once had for myself became my dream for them. I wanted my children to grow up in a home that was peaceful. I wanted my house to look and feel like it was lived in by a happy, busy family. My sister used to tell me that even though she had a house, my place always felt like home to her. Her feelings filled my heart. I made it a point to fill my walls with decorations and pictures that reflected affection and tenderness. I wanted to impart love, acceptance, and peace to all who entered my home.

My home was the perfect haven that I'd always imagined it would be, but I continued to embark on trips to the places of my childhood dreams. One of my frequent destinations is a luxury villa that was built in the waters around Bora Bora. It floats on the most beautiful aquamarine-blue ocean that you could ever imagine. The masterfully designed master suite provides access for my feet to transition directly from my bed to the warm tropical waters as the cool morning breeze greets me.

Though this place exists only in my dreams, I can feel with every fiber of my being how peaceful and quiet it will be to just lay across that bed and listen to the stillness as the bluest waters crash against the rocks in the private cove. I can feel my body rocking back and forth as the waves would billow up then down, washing all my worries away and cooling my body in their spray. While this setting remains a dream much like many of my childhood escapes, I am thrilled that I'm able to create my own peace in my own home as my escape today.

Peace and comfort may have finally found me as I have come to settle into the home that I prepared for my girls. I was able to give us the sort of place where they and others are welcome, and they can receive unconditional love, respect, and acceptance. I have a place where, no matter how old they are, they know it's safe to just lay in their mommy's bed and the world, just for that moment, will stand still. I hold them during times like these and allow them to cry, laugh, or just be silent in the peaceful place I've created called home.

I also realized that the place of my childhood dreams was now a place of my family's reality.

1. **Where is your place of peace?**
2. **Was it provided for you, or did you have to create it?**
3. **What will it take for you to maintain that peace?**

A Moment To Reflect

Creativity

When I walked into the room, my creativity was activated. There was so much beauty surrounding me and so many things to see. In that moment, it was clearly my destiny to be in this room full of artists displaying the best parts of themselves. This group of talented individuals could take simple objects and turn them into beautiful, amazing creations. As I strolled through the room, to my left were portraits of beautiful black regal families embodying the picture of success, sitting on fancy couches and perched to perfection. These strong, noble black families brought joy to my soul. Seeing our heritage of kings and queens on display in such a modern and real way gave me hope. To my right was an artist who had displayed beautiful statues of birds that had been crafted to perfection. He stood in front of them proudly in his three-piece suit and tennis shoes. I didn't even know his name, but I loved this artist for his confidence and sense of style. In the far corner was a woman who was painting a landscape that was full of small brush strokes and loads of color. Watching the painting develop in front of my eyes held my attention in a soothing way. I was amazed that while she was covered in paint, her hair was beautifully natural, and she was relaxed in her jeans and loafers. I don't know why her outfit caught my eye, but it seemed so genuine and unique.

Then I noticed my spot. I had set up a booth with a sign that read, "Give me a word and in five minutes I will develop a story based off of your aura and what vibes I pick up from your presence." I had done these many times before at events, and it was always a hit. It wasn't hard for me to find words and make something beautiful out of them. I am an artist and words are my medium. Each of the artists in the room was telling a story without words. They were expressing themselves in their purest form. I felt at home amongst my artist tribe.

When the doors opened and people started to flood in, it seemed like chaos had broken out. There were so many different types of people packed in this one area—mostly African American people since this was a cultural event that was geared toward black love and acceptance. This event was a showcase of creativity, culture, and independence. The first word I was given was from a distinguished older gentleman wearing a bow tie, vest, and blue jeans. The word he gave me was "emerging." I looked him up and down and had him turn in a circle slowly, then walk in front of me for a few steps. Then I confidently told him that I had his story.

His story went like this:

> As he emerged from the darkness that was his younger years, he decided his path would be one that no one had experienced yet. If you were lucky enough to be in his presence, it meant that you had something that he wanted, whether it be knowledge, money, prestige, or just conversation. He took in no simpletons, as he was a statement in his own right. He loved hard and adorned himself with things that only he understood and appreciated. He allowed no one to ever diminish his light, as it was the very thing that allowed him to see into the dark recesses of his mind. His career could not be reduced to a title and his experiences could not be captured in a story. He was more—more style, more grace, more love, more expression, and less words, worry, or care. He is his own type of person, and no one anywhere is going to place him in a box. His joy is beyond those that he encounters, and his soul is one to be adored. He is Emerging!!

I read the piece out loud to the crowd as the line began to form in front of me. Tears began to stream down his face as he took in my words. He told me that no one had ever really understood him. He went on to explain that from the time he was a young boy, people never really "saw" him, but I had seen him perfectly and clearly in just five minutes. He thanked me, handed me a $100 bill for my work and left. I love who I am and what I do for people with my words. That day I wrote over thirty stories to add to my collection. I was fulfilling my calling and it fueled my soul.

1. **What creative gift or talent are you not using?**

2. **What can you do to explore more of your gifts and talents?**

A Moment To Reflect

Growth

The growth that I saw in her was amazing!

She had told me specifically that she was not ready for this journey. She said she had too many obstacles and not enough time, was in a bad head space, and her relationship was screwed up. I listened to all her concerns and told her that we could start this journey right where she was. She didn't need to make any sudden adjustments. All that was required were small, strategic steps to better the parts of her life that were causing her to feel stuck.

First, we talked about her goals and what she needed and wanted out of life. She said she wanted to be happy. I asked her, "What does your happiness look like?" She began to tell me it was living with less stress, more room to think clearly, and a partner who understands her and is a great communicator. As she talked, I smiled inwardly. I had been in her shoes many times in my life, but I knew my path to resolution was not the solution to hers.

We broke down each section of her life that she wanted to address and made an action plan of changes that would move her closer to her goals and further from her pain. She explained to me that she had, over the last year, gained sixty pounds and it was weighing on her mentally and physically. She explained that with the problems and pain came the weight, and that if she could release some of the weight some of her problems would also be offloaded.

I told her that sounded reasonable and asked what she would like to do to move toward that goal. Almost too quickly she told me that she didn't have much time to work out and that she refused to go to a gym. Hearing her fears, I asked if there was anything she could do in the neighborhood or at home that would help her move more each day. She said that she could walk around the neighborhood to start. I told her that was a great idea and asked how much time she could commit each day. She said, "I can squeeze in an hour." I was impressed by her enthusiasm to start aggressively, but I figured that smaller steps would give her a better chance of long-term success. We then agreed to avoid feeling overwhelmed, she would begin with a thirty-minute walk. I then told her that if she felt like more and had time, then she could walk farther; but for the time being, a commitment of thirty minutes was a better start than the burden of an hour. She agreed.

I asked, "What else do you think you can do to assist with your weight release?" She suggested giving up breakfast, stating that she was never really hungry in the morning. I told her, "Let's not take anything away, so how about we add more water to your diet instead? Let's commit to one hundred ounces of water a day. I know it sounds like a lot, but if you drink a cup an hour, it is really not that bad. Let's give it a try and see how many days you can accomplish this." She liked that idea.

I also added to her list to think about one positive thing during her walk while envisioning what she wanted her future to look like, and suggested using the prompt of "What would a perfect day look like for you?" She already knew the answer, and said, "Sixty pounds lighter, a partner to work out with, and an organized business filled with happy customers free of stress." I agreed that that did sound like a perfect day, and said, "Okay, so let's start envisioning that while you're walking each day for thirty minutes."

After setting the plan in motion I suggested we meet again in two weeks to see how things were going. When she arrived, it was so clear she was in good spirits that I had to comment about how she seemed to be glowing. She told me how great she felt and that she had even lost five pounds. "Five pounds—what? That's a great start!" I told her. As we reviewed her accomplishments over the previous two weeks, she told me that she walked for thirty to forty-five minutes a day and was drinking more water. She said she was more surprised at how visualizing her perfect day really improved her mood.

"The first week while I was walking, I met a lady who walks around the same time as I do. She and I have been walking together and I really like it. We don't talk, we just walk, and I visualize my life the way I want it. Knowing she will be waiting makes me want to jump up each morning and see her. Usually at the end of our walk we talk a little. She's really nice."

"Wow, so you found a partner to work out with already? That is awesome," I told her.

When I asked her about the water consumption, she said she struggled to get one hundred ounces but could usually get in at least sixty-four. I told her, "That's a great start. Just keep up the good work." That day she left me with a few more action items and a great attitude. I realized during that visit that if she continued to make small steps toward her goal, she would walk right into that new vision of her life. Her growth and transformation were inspiring to me, so that afternoon I took my vision for a walk. For the next few days I continued to do my vision walk again and again and now I better understand how she had said her body felt lighter. With growth comes a lighter heart and a brighter future.

1. **In what areas of your life have you grown?**
2. **Have you celebrated while continually pushing yourself?**
3. **Who have you encouraged lately?**
4. **Seek someone out and shine a little of your light on them.**

A Moment To Reflect

Positive

I could feel the positive energy emitting from the room. The sun was just dawning, but for some reason I felt a presence that made me light up from the inside out. What a wonderful feeling—just knowing that something that you cannot see or hear has such an impact on your mood. For some reason the sunlight that flooded the room seemed to be so bright and so was my heart. My heart felt light and full of possibilities and endless opportunities for the day ahead. It was sure to be an amazing day. Why was this day special? Who knows, but it was! It was not knowing what the day would bring but an intention being sent out into the universe that filled me with such comfort—a beckoning for this day to be all that it was called to be.

As the crisp air blew through my window and the smell of freshly cut grass tickled my nose, all I could see was green. Green to me signifies positive energy, a renewal of one's spirit, a regeneration of wealth, a reuniting of families. I felt that if I could simply align all the stars in my life, I would have the power to place everything where it should be on this day: relationships, love, career, happiness, purpose, joy—they were all at the tip of my fingers that day. All I had to do was embrace it and call it so.

Have you ever felt that way? Have you ever realized that you had the world at your fingertips and all you had to do is grab hold of it and everything would fall into place? I hope you have, because there are not enough words in the dictionary to explain what I was feeling on that magnificent, glorious, perfect morning. Thinking of the shift such a day could bring made my heart skip a beat.

The perfect song for this moment was "God Favored Me." I believe God favors me and extends his grace and mercy to my life in a consistent and loving manner. No matter what the obstacle, if I wait long enough, things will always work out for my good. That is how my God works. This day I felt a shift in the atmosphere, and I was excited to see what God had reserved for me. I had butterflies in my tummy and a deep knowing that I was being set up for greatness beyond my wildest dreams. As a matter of fact, what I realized is that my dreams were too small for that moment. I had been selling myself and my purpose short. I needed to dream bigger, do more, build alliances, and connect with mentors, because this new season I was stepping into cannot be entered into alone. I know I have God, but he has also placed people on this earth to work with me to define moments like this: a magnificent, glowing, dewy, crisp-white-shirt kind of brilliant morning. Now let's go out there and seize the day!

1. **Do you have a positive outlook on life?**

2. **How do you declare and set the atmosphere for your day?**

3. **What are you looking forward to?**

A Moment To Reflect

_____

_____

_____

_____

_____

_____

_____

_____

_____

_____

Butterfly

It was a butterfly that altered my life.

The captivating beauty, the brilliance of the colors, defeating insurmountable odds to get to this place, the humblest of beginnings. It was the life cycle of the butterfly that showed me what I can become if I simply trust the process.

As a child I lived in deep poverty. We called it "the projects" in Baltimore City. It was where nobody seemed to care about their homes. There were drug dealers and addicts on every corner. My family lived in a high-rise that looked over the city. From the windows of our apartment all I could see was trash, crime, and people living lives of hopelessness, just as a caterpillar only has a view from the ground when crawling on its belly and is never able to see more than a few inches in front of him. Walking those sidewalks of my neighborhood, all I felt was empty and lost. No one seemed to be trying to get out of there. No one seemed to want better. The feelings of depression and despair were everywhere, just like the trash that littered the street. I knew I didn't belong there. As the hours, days, and years went by, I got older and began to forge my own path.

I was trying to do something different to make my life better when no one around me seemed to be doing it. Making the change was a long and lonely road. Choosing to go to school and educate myself so I could have a brighter future seemed crazy to those around me. Working full-time, going to school full-time, and being a full-time mom left no time for fun. No one understood my choice to take the hard road. Many times, my family and friends would refuse to watch my children or help out by lending me money to pay for school. They didn't understand why I was not at the clubs and instead was at home studying, so I simply stayed to myself, much like the stage in which the caterpillar goes into a cocoon. Wrapped in a cocoon, it cannot see the outside world yet waits quietly, believing that one day it will be released from the darkness and be set free.-

Then finally it was time to graduate, like breaking out of a cocoon and finally experiencing freedom. With this new life came home buying, children succeeding, and new opportunities that exceeded my wildest dreams, all because I'd endured the darkness and embraced change. I had arrived! My dreams had emerged. Now I could make choices from options instead of necessity. It was glorious.

When I got my wings my perspective about life changed while others around me remained the same. Years later they were still walking those same sidewalks, partying, and complaining about how life done them wrong. I relocated not only my life but my thinking. I bought a home in the country with trees and beautiful grass and lovely surroundings instead of chaos on every corner. I was free to move about the world. Just as the butterfly emerges from the cocoon as a beautiful creature, my future filled with new opportunities was more beautiful than I could have imagined. I had made it out of darkness, my steps felt lighter, and I now saw hope where I used to see only hopelessness.

The funny thing about butterflies is they can't see how beautiful their wings are. Just like that butterfly, it took me a while to see my magnificent wings. Sometimes, I don't even realize how far I've traveled from where I began. I didn't realize how dark my world was until I stood in the light. Although some days it takes more effort to see my wings, the fact remains that I am a butterfly and I am designed to fly.

1. **Are you experiencing challenges in your pursuit of a better life?**

2. **What stage are you experiencing in your life right now?**

3. **Have you given yourself credit for overcoming so much darkness to finally see the light?**

A Moment To Reflect

_____

_____

_____

_____

_____

_____

_____

_____

_____

_____

_____

_____

_____

_____

_____

_____

_____

_____

Ambiguous

Every time I asked my coach a question, her responses were ambiguous.

I mean, she could have taken the time to explain exactly what she meant by "Time is going to pass no matter what you do." I kept telling her over and over again that I am a major procrastinator. Procrastination may not work for everyone, but it seemed to be working fine for me. I have done it my entire life. Then comes this high-priced life coach who was getting on my last nerve. I wanted her to take a seat and just tell me the next step. But she claimed I was not finished with the step I was currently on. Okay, I admit I did the dang business plan half-assed, but I did it. Ain't it her job to make sure it's right, or did I hire the wrong person? The more I blurted out the endless tasks that needed to be completed, the more she pushed me to organize my thoughts and write them down. So, begrudgingly I started the action plan just to get her off my back. She kept telling me this would serve as a guide for my business plan, goals, and action steps. Boy, was she right!

Seeing it mapped out on paper made me less anxious and more productive. Finally! I wasn't overwhelmed because I knew exactly what needed to be done and the steps to get there. I felt a shift that caused me to start connecting to like-minded people that positively impacted me and my business. I was excited about reaching the next step and realized my procrastination was rooted in fear of having to get so much done.

As my mindset began to change, I started seeing my coach as an encourager and a partner who wanted to see me succeed. I began to embrace and value her input. We would review my lists and assign priorities to every item. I couldn't believe that the work that I had dreaded ultimately made the process as a whole much easier. My coach kept me focused, continuously checked on me, and pulled me up when I began to backslide into my sedentary ways. She had become my cheerleader at a time when I needed it most. I never could have paid her enough money for her guidance, expertise, and ability to hold me accountable. Because of her and her "nagging," I now have a successful business that has purpose and a vision. Because of her I am feeling less stress, making great money, and helping people. What a blessing she has been to my life.

In the end, it wasn't about the money I spent, it was about my investment in listening, learning, focusing, and doing what is required to achieve my goals. Failing to make that investment was the reason my business was not thriving, and my coach taught me how to make my business prosper. Even though I fought some of the steps, mapping out a plan, setting a vision, and following through were the keys to my success, and I owe it all to her.

1. **Take a moment to write down your next goal, then write a list of tasks.**

2. **After you complete a task, check it off and celebrate how far you have come.**

3. **Find a person that will keep you accountable and share your list of tasks and accomplishments with them.**

A Moment To Reflect

_____

_____

_____

_____

_____

_____

_____

_____

_____

_____

_____

_____

_____

_____

_____

_____

_____

_____

Build

When many people hear the word "build," they often think of home construction. When I think of the word build, my soul smiles and reflects on the building up of myself or others.

I have always been a builder of sorts. I love to feed positivity into people's lives and, dare I say, "convince" them to believe in themselves. As a young child, I lacked words of affirmation. Maybe that is why I try to give what I lacked for so long. When my children were young, I constantly told them that they could do anything if they put their minds to it. I don't know if I necessarily believed it at the time, but I wanted them to believe they could live their wildest dreams without a doubt.

Because of motivational speakers like Eric Thomas and Lisa Nichols, I have gotten better at taking a no-nonsense approach to helping people get out of their own way and realize the greatness inside them. What I have seen is that people are always picking themselves apart, leaving very little to build upon. I try to get them to recall the amazing parts of their story. Though past circumstances may only allow someone to recall the negative, self-deprecating, soul-stealing parts of their story, I believe we need to focus on the amazing, triumphant, and resilient parts of our story.

If I could go back and teach myself one thing, it would be to accept and love who I am, and to always remember that I am a warrior, I am a work in progress, and I am a light that imparts positive energy to myself and others.

Eric Thomas says, "There is greatness upon you," and we must believe that truth and build on it. Today, I ask you to choose to see the beauty within you and build, or dare I say rebuild, that better version of you.

1. What do you believe about yourself, and how can you build a more positive vision of that person?

2. Make a list of your most admirable attributes and why you love them.

A Moment To Reflect

_____

_____

_____

_____

_____

_____

_____

_____

_____

_____

_____

_____

_____

_____

Annoyed

That girl annoyed the hell out of me! I tried so hard to keep my distance from her, but it seemed no matter what I did she always seemed to find me. She is the type of person who speaks loudly, has to be seen, and is always making excuses for her behavior. I can't stand being around someone that is so loud and needy.

I had been Sandra's friend for over ten years. We used to hang out in elementary school on the playground, and she was my only true friend, and I was hers. I am not sure what brought us together—maybe we were just different enough to be alike. I didn't really like to be around too many people and Sandra seemed lonely as people picked on her constantly. Maybe it was the large black mole on her nose. Kids would say it was her honker as they tried to push it to see if it would make noise. Sandra would swat their hands away and call them names, but that never stopped them from trying. As she got older, she became more aggressive and shorter tempered with people. She would talk about people and make fun of them in order to hurt them before they could hurt her. She would not back down if someone tried to talk back to her; instead, she would get more defensive and sometimes it would end in a fight. By the end of seventh grade, she was really good at fighting, but the kids still picked on her. I thought it was funny because they had so much mouth and then when she put her books down, they would say, "I was just playing."

Sandra got the mole removed during her junior year of high school. She had always been a beautiful girl, but now that the mole was gone, OMG, she was stunning. She started wearing makeup and her beauty silenced all those who had once made fun of her. Something changed and something remained the same. Sandra continued to bully. It was like the bullied became the bully. One day I pulled her aside as she was really being hard on a girl who had buck teeth. I said to her, "Why are you bullying her? She can't help how her teeth look. Don't you remember what it felt like when people would pick on you?" She said, "Yeah, I do, and it's my turn now." I didn't understand her reasoning, so I decided to distance myself from her. She asked me one day, "Why are you acting so funny? You act like you don't want to hang out anymore." I said, "Because I don't. I don't like the way you talk to people. You're cruel, rude, and loud. I don't want people to think that I'm anything like you, so I choose to separate myself from you." She looked at me with tears streaming down her face and she walked away.

I was shocked! What just happened? Was I wrong to say that? Did I hurt her feelings? Was I now the bad person? I followed her into the girls' bathroom and tapped her on the shoulder and asked, "What's up?" She said, "I never want to lose you as a friend. I know that I can be mean, and I feel like people made me that way. I'm loud because I don't want people to judge me or say evil things to me. In all the world, you are the last person I want to lose." She said, "You have been my friend through all of my difficult times and the only person that truly stood up or tried to understand me. I am sorry and I will try to change. Losing you as a friend is not worth the tough exterior that I have built to try and keep myself from getting hurt." We hugged right there in the bathroom. What I learned that day changed me. I realized that hurt people, hurt people. It's funny how, if you have been in an awful situation, you would think you would want to spare others from having the same experience, but Sandra did the opposite.

I hate the walls that we have to build around ourselves in order to deal with life's difficulties. I wish that everyone was seen as a person and the character that they embody, not for what they look like. When Sandra was young, her experiences hardened her and caused her to build this really defensive person that wanted to hurt others before she could be hurt. Deep inside, all she wanted was acceptance and someone to be nice to her. I think we should all aspire to be kind and accepting to those that need kindness.

1. **Are you allowing past experiences to define who you are today?**

2. **How can you get back to the true authentic you, the one before the trauma?**

A Moment To Reflect

Change

Change is inevitable.

Life is all about change. If you want to survive, you have to change. One benefit of change is that you get the privilege of seeing things from a different perspective. Change gives you the opportunity to appreciate a different mindset.

Most of the changes in my life have come from either calculated moves or tragedies. One of the calculated moves was using education to provide a better life for my kids. Yes, these changes required making hard decisions. Yes, these changes forced me to step out of my comfort zone and do things that others around me were not doing. Going to college instead of just accepting a job was new territory. I decided that even though no one around me, including anyone in my family, had gone to college, I wanted a better life for myself and my kids. And as foreign as it felt going to college, I knew it was the answer. I had to work all day and go to school several nights a week. I had to take the train instead of driving because it allowed me more time to study. Nothing came easy. It was grueling but I did it because I wanted to create a change. During those twelve long years people told me I was crazy, they didn't want to help me with my kids, and I was going so long I "should be a doctor by now."

To further ensure my kids were set up for success, I moved us to a more affluent area that I chose by reviewing the school rankings. I knew I could not afford private school but paying higher rent was something I could do. I also decided to put them in dance class from the time they were three years old because I wanted them to be engaged in activities outside of school. "No idle hands in my house" was the family motto. Another family motto was "We don't quit, we pivot."

After my oldest daughter quit her dance classes, she pivoted to singing. My two youngest played basketball. My middle daughter also played the violin. Our home was always in forward growth motion. I wanted them to be better, so I had to do better. I had to show them that we do not quit, and that even though it was a long road, the outcome had to be a degree. I believed the outcome of all the extra effort that I'd put into them and myself would lead to success. The girls are now healthy, whole, driven women. They believe they can do anything they put their minds to. My determination to change the narrative of my life into something different also changed theirs. Change often creates other changes. When you change the way you look at things, the things you look at change!

1. **What bold change do you need to make?**

2. **How has change worked for you in the past?**

3. **Are you willing to pay the price that change is going to require?**

4. **What is your biggest fear around change?**

A Moment To Reflect

High Hopes

I have high hopes for my future.

I catch myself sitting back and envisioning what I want this world to look like from my perspective. I don't know if it's called forecasting or manifesting, but it sure does make me feel good. I focus on all my wildest dreams coming true, like traveling to foreign countries and seeing beautiful sites, sitting all day with friends, and just relaxing or having a glass of wine at sunset on a tropical island. It seems so many people have no real vision for their future, so as a result their outlook may seem bleak, dull, and very black-and-white.

Me, I see my future in full color. I imagine full panoramic views of oceans and huts floating on the water where I put my feet in the water without leaving my bed. My vision is filled with beautiful sunrises, sunsets, and amazing scenery, and is full to the brim with new adventures. Yeah, my future is bright, and my life is vibrant and in living color. Any time I get depressed and struggle with seeing the good in things, I just remind myself that this situation is just for a moment. My real life is on its way. Yes!! Greater is always around the corner if you are looking for it.

I love who I am and what I have to offer this world. I give positive energy, laughs, love, headaches, and heartaches, but mostly good things. You can't have the good without the bad. I used to think I was all bad, but I have made up my mind that though my past had some really great episodes, my future has the best of my life to come.

It's a good thing I don't have to pay for the high hopes for my future because the money comes with the setting. I gain as I go along because I feel no lack in my perfect place. I feel loads of abundance, love, wealth, friends, family, and success. Dang, currently I am experiencing much of that, but how will it be when

I finally reach my desired destination? I could not imagine being happier than I am right now, but I know it is possible. I speak all things into existence, I am a bad-ass woman, and I get what I manifest.

1. **What are you currently manifesting in your life, whether consciously or subconsciously?**
2. **Do you believe you can speak things into existence?**

A Moment To Reflect

_____

_____

_____

_____

_____

_____

_____

_____

_____

_____

_____

_____

_____

Love is Stupid

Love is so stupid. Somehow it makes you do crazy things like hooking up with people that you don't really like.

Love causes you to risk your peace and ignore your inner voice. Love somehow convinces you that you love a person with all of your heart without knowing their middle name. Love makes a knock upside the head feel like a love tap while telling you to understand that "he needed to release some stress from a really bad day at work." Love leaves you mindless. Love tells you that you want to be with someone no matter how they treat you. Love overrides everything that is logical.

A friend of mine wanted to marry her longtime boyfriend. He was a horrible person. He even had multiple children with other women while they were together. He had left her when she was about to be evicted and treated her like she was disposable even though she always made sure he had a place to stay and food to eat. One day my friend told me she was getting married to this man, and I had to ask her, "Why?" She said, "Because of all the hell he put me through, he owes it to me." I said, "What does he owe you—more misery, more heartache, more pain?" I could not understand why she wanted to connect her life to his. Then I realized that she somehow thought that a little piece of paper would make it better. Without missing a beat she said, "I just want what he owes me."

I said, "He has been giving you what he owes you: absolutely nothing. And now you want to add marriage to all that dysfunction?" It seemed ridiculously crazy to me, but I have done some pretty outrageous, stupid things because of love, so who was I to judge?

I married a man that was completely crazy and clinically unstable at times. He was the most caring, loving, kind gentlemen, but he had a horrible temper and used his words to destroy anything and anybody that didn't agree with him. He became another person when he was angry. I believe he was bipolar, but I married him anyway. Why the hell would someone with good sense, which is what I claim to have, mess with someone so toxic? Love. I felt he needed love and that I had enough love to heal all the bad things inside of him. Man, was I wrong! He eventually ended up leaving me and doing some irreparable damage to my self-esteem and self-confidence, all in the name of love. Even after all that he did, I wanted to love him again and try to move past the hurt and pain. Well, everyone knows that never works. And yet here I was telling my friend, "Don't be dumb," while wearing the big-ass dunce hat that I'd proudly paraded around in for seven years.

Yeah, it's funny how stupid we can be for love—that thing that is so fleeting and never really stays around long. Love can be something so deep and perfect and yet we take it so lightly and use the word all willy-nilly and equally, like "I love this pizza" and "I love my children." How does that make sense? We need more than one word to express that feeling we call love. But that's just life—we use a lot of words and terms out of context to fit our narrative. We do the same thing with the Bible. We read some parts and take the words and force them to fit into our story and not us into it. We pretend to hold ourselves to the great Scriptures like "God has a plan for your life," but we're just good at reciting the parts we like and that make us feel good. We act like His plan is always for happiness and sunshine. But some of those plans feel really messed up. They lead to heartbreak, lost love and loved ones, failures, disappointments, and a whole host of other things. And in the middle of all that, the Bible has the nerve to tell you not to lose heart over trials and tribulations. Really, God? Are you going to really tell me to not be mad because this man that I gave my whole heart to because I felt You told me to literally tried to destroy the fabric of who I am as a person? And then you take away 50 percent of my family in just five short months and you didn't think I was going to lose heart. Shoot, I didn't even think at that point I had a heart. How is that love?

But then you tell me joy comes in the morning. Well, can you tell me what morning it's going to show up? I really need joy to bring his tail on so I can get my happy on. I need you to move out of the way so I can get my love back. If you love me, instead of finding me trials, find me joy. And just when time heals some of the pain and you decide to let someone in, then you fail at love again. So yes, I think that love is stupid.

But what is the alternative: no love? A loveless, empty life? One filled with only the bad and never the good? No, I am sorry to say I don't care how stupid love is, I will take love and all of its euphoria, bliss, peace, happiness, calmness, connection, and laughter that comes with it for as long as I can. Love is a choice, and I chose to indulge—even if it often does not choose me.

1. **How have your experiences with love shaped your views on love?**
2. **And do you believe that God (or a higher being) can use your pain for a purpose, and why?**

A Moment To Reflect

Mockery

They always seem to make a mockery out of me. As hard as I try to keep my composure and not be the brunt of someone's joke, *they* always seem to find me funny and want to make fun of me. It is not fun, and I have tried to learn to deal with it all. I have been polite. I refined my spoken voice to nearly perfect English diction, but *they* called me stuck up and suggested I remove the stick from my ass. I tried to explain to them that I had worked really hard to get rid of my accent and communicate fluidly like my Caucasian counterparts, but it didn't matter—*they* had chosen something about me to mock and nothing I said would end their attacks. I know *they* will never be able to go into spaces that I will be welcomed into. *They* may be smart, but since I have the power of words at my command, I will get the job long before they get an interview. I will probably end up being their boss and yet *they* will continue to tell me that I sound weird.

Well, forget them. I am who I am, and I refuse to allow those people to make me feel bad about myself and who I am. I will write my own ticket and build my own business and make millions. I will choose to see the good in people and not find ways to mock them and make them feel small so I can feel tall. Yeah, unique is what I am, and today I will not allow them to dull my shine. I am one of a kind. I am an original; there is no one like me and that is what I choose to believe about myself. It does not matter that *they* don't want to be my friends. I'll stay to myself. None of that matters because what is viewed as a joke today will lead me to my destiny of greatness—a destiny filled with lavish homes, luxury cars, friends, extravagant vacations, and high-profile businesses. I choose to focus on my future instead of on them. I will have the last laugh and *they* will see that, instead of becoming like them, I went high when they went low, and as a result, I rose high. I will gladly watch them get smaller in my rearview mirror as I progress toward greatness!

1. **Who are *they* in your life?**

2. **What do *they* say about you that is untrue?**

3. Why do you choose to let *them* define you and your greatness?

4. Who do you need to remove from your circle?

A Moment To Reflect

_____

_____

_____

_____

_____

_____

_____

_____

_____

_____

_____

_____

_____

_____

_____

On the Grid

It's funny how people are always on the grid and never disconnecting, yet never making real connections, never taking time for themselves.

I love taking time off from the grid. Taking a timeout from social media, fake friends, work, and just resting and being me can be a good thing. I have been led to believe that in today's world we have to always be in a state of connectedness—yet that need to always be connected has caused our society to be the most disconnected. We have started putting people on a pedestal based on manicured profiles and the number of followers they have. We think that we are not cut from the same cloth as they are because we continually compare what we have to what we see of them on TV or social media. The truth is it takes a long time and hard work for a singer or actor to make money; and if they catch up with success, it is well deserved. Overnight, viral fame is not the same as well-earned success.

Trying to live your life through someone else's eyes can be extremely difficult, if not impossible. Most of the lives that people allow you to see are smoke and mirrors. They are made-up images to impress strangers and often exclude the truth. The standard of pretty has been altered into unreal expectations because of the makeup, weaves, and filters. Yeah, it's easy to have a bigger ass and fuller lips when you have the app (or surgery) to make it happen. And when you are a star, it is even easier to look amazing when you have a team of experts that are trained to make you look that way. But is it the real you? Or is the real you the one that is caught on the streets looking like a homeless person?

Sometimes I feel sad because I neglect to see the beauty in what I have accomplished. I forget where I came from and only see where I have yet to arrive. How crazy is that? How self-absorbed do you have to be in other people's lives not to realize that you have come so incredibly far, and that you do not need half of the stuff that you swear you need to make you "feel better"? I should be able to feed off my accomplishments for the rest of my life. I have changed the fabric of who I am and have chosen to raise children that are breaking generational curses and building legacies. I claim that! I don't need ten thousand likes to know that I have done a good job; I don't need five thousand followers to appreciate my new car. All I need is to love and be proud of who I am. Comparison is the thief of joy and accomplishments. When you spend your time comparing yourself to others, you will always be disappointed, and you will always feel inadequate, insufficient, and small. You can't beat someone else at being them, but you can damn sure be the best version of who you are without a doubt.

If people expect Lisa Nichols or Sarah Jakabs when I show up, they will be upset because I will always show up as me. But if they come to see Trina, then they have set themselves up for a great treat because this woman right here has accomplished some great feats and has done some amazing things with her life. She pulled herself up by the bootstraps and stomped right out of poverty into a plan—a plan that not only elevates her life but elevates the lives of those that come after her. She is a superhero in her own right and no amount of comparison can steal that!

1. **When is the last time you got disconnected from the world and took a break?**

2. **What are you most proud of in who you are?**

3. **When was the last time you celebrated just being you?**

A Moment To Reflect

_____

_____

_____

_____

_____

_____

_____

_____

_____

_____

_____

_____

_____

_____

_____

_____

_____

_____

Rash

The uncomfortableness I was experiencing could have been a rash, but I think it was deeper than that. I was becoming so irritated with whatever it was that I continued to keep focused on the problem and not the goal. I am not sure what brought this "rash" on, but I needed to figure it out and then get rid of it. Was I the cause? I didn't want to be. I wanted to be the solution. The solution is always better than the cause. I want to be the solution to all problems that young women experience when they need guidance and a mother figure to talk to, to keep them engaged, to hold them accountable, and to make them feel loved. But how? How could I possibly accomplish such a thing? I had been trying extremely hard to get this dream of being that person for others off the ground. I had been hell-bent on finding a way for F.E.M.E Work to reach young women. But I had lost hope and needed some direction. I knew I was the cure to the problem, but I didn't know how to get the business world to realize that they needed this program for their clients to be successful. I could not for the life of me figure it out, but I knew there had to be a way. I knew that in all things there is a solution. So, what next? I knew I had to keep talking. I knew I had to keep promoting. I knew I had to keep moving and not sit out on my dream.

But is it possible to have such a desire inside you and never see it realized? How can you have thousands of resources right at your fingertips and they never grow to the potential of being an asset? They don't even know they need me. I have to keep reminding myself that they don't know, and I need to find a way to make them know. I remember someone once told me, "You don't know what you don't know." And that is the biggest problem for me. I have the material but not the stage to deliver it. What part of the platform am I missing? I know I am the answer; I know it. I need to figure out what organizations are out there trying to find the answer that is me. I know there is a group of young women that want someone to make them better, to help them become more accountable, to teach them how to move strategically toward their goals.

Maybe the answer is I don't have to be the whole solution. Maybe if I helped the people already helping people then that will allow me to be a part of the solution, even if it is not on my stage but someone else's. I am not the rash; I am a healing salve that is just part of the solution. That's what I choose to believe. Now, let me go find my tribe!

1. **Evaluate what your pain points have been in life and develop a plan to help those that have the same pain.**

2. **How are you going to help those who don't even realize they need your help?**

3. **Who do you know that already has a stage you can share?**

A Moment To Reflect

_____

_____

_____

_____

_____

_____

_____

_____

_____

_____

$\mathcal{P}eak$

It was at the peak of my career that I realized where I was may not be a good fit for me.

I always wondered who I would be if I decided to live my dream and not hide in the shadows of others. Up to this point, I had spent most of my career supporting C-Level executives. Yes, it was nice to be seated at the top of the organizational chart, but at what cost? I basically organized their lives. I scheduled their meetings, I moved their doctors' appointments, I dressed them for conferences, and rehearsed their speeches for top-level meetings. You can say I did it all. I always wanted to be an executive assistant and I was going to be the best at it no matter what. My job was very fulfilling, and I had many people who counted on me and believed in my ability to get the job done. Because of my position I carried the authority of the person I was supporting, and I knew how to use it.

After years of lifting others into success I realized I did not want to be the one just scheduling the meetings, but the person running them. I wanted to add value inside the room by making the big decisions instead of outside the room making the coffee. I felt like I had more in me and that I was not living up to my potential. The trap was the jobs paid me well, and just about the time I was ready to walk away I was promoted to a higher level and compensated with higher pay. Where I worked was great, the people treated me well, and I had the ear of top executives. I went from working for directors, to assistant deans, to deans, to vice presidents.

To make the shift, I knew I had to adjust to not having the authority of a top executive behind me. I felt like I needed to alter my approach when interacting with people because my position had changed. But what I realized is that I didn't need their authority because I had my own. I had made a reputation for myself, and it followed me regardless of the position I was in. My strengths were rooted in the relationships I had built, the skills I had cultivated, and the positive attitude

I embodied. My name was recognized and respected and I had influence that degrees or highfalutin titles couldn't get me.

All along I thought my success was based on who I worked for and not who I was and what I could accomplish. I realized that my true value was not dependent on the person I was supporting, it was in the fabric of who I am.

1. **Are you giving credit to others for your success?**
2. **How are you valuing who you are in your current position in life?**

A Moment To Reflect

_____

_____

_____

_____

_____

_____

_____

_____

_____

_____

_____

_____

Heat

When I think of heat, I think of a woman I know and the passion she exudes when entering a room. She was told that since she was passionate about her children, about her man, and about her life, then her name should be Passion. And thus the hot, fierce, and mysterious biker chick was born.

She liked to be noticed, and there was an air about her that made her presence known when she stepped into a room. When Passion rode her motorcycle, she felt free and uninhibited. She made up her mind long ago that no matter what was happening around her, she owned her position on her bike and in her life. Her all-leather attire and biker chic vibe, coupled with the badass butterfly tattoo on her back, gave her the appearance of a tough girl, which masked the warmth of her gentle heart. Passion was full of love, so it came as no surprise to learn that she had a calling to motivate and inspire people.

Passion loved to uplift people and make them see the good in themselves. It was her superpower and she used it for the good of all who crossed her path. Everything about Passion intrigued me. I was certain that mine was only one of many lives that she touched. I signed up to attend one of her seminars unsure what to expect, but I knew I needed to know more about this woman and the source of her confidence.

That day she referred to herself as Trina, but from the attention her presence commanded as she entered the stage, I was certain that she was indeed the Passion I knew from the bike club. She explained that when she first began her journey to self-discovery, she used to have a negative view of herself. She used the letters of her name to define how she felt: **T** for timid, **R** for regretful, **I** for insecure, **N** for naïve, and **A** for angry. The audience was captivated by her story of redemption as she explained how she started by owning her own voice and living her life on her own terms. She redefined herself and decided to own who she was, which changed the meaning of her name to: **T** for tenacious, **R** for resilient, **I** for inspiring, **N** for no-nonsense, and **A** for affirming.

Trina did not stop there; she challenged us to do the same with our names. She explained how it was important that our names have meaning, because if we decide who we are for ourselves, then we won't allow anyone to reduce us to less than we see of ourselves. Her talk that day was FIRE! I could feel the same heat coming from her as I could when she was on her motorcycle. I was astonished!

That afternoon I realized that there is always more than one layer to people—in fact, there are more layers than most of us can imagine. Seeing Passion own her life made me an instant fan (maybe even a little stalker-ish). I began to mimic her moves. I would stand taller, speak louder, and focus more on the woman in the mirror. I made it my mission to redefine who I was and what I had been called to do. After a while, I was no longer mimicking Passion—I had become the authentic version of the person I was called to be.

I am both Trina and Passion. I assure you that if you take a look in the mirror, you also will see the confident, beautiful, and amazing person that you admire trying to come through. Doubt is the killer of all good things, so by having faith and deciding to step into and own the person that you wish to be, you can achieve greatness. I hope you discover the Passion inside of you like I did, so you can finally allow that bad-ass, heat-driven, red-hot rock star with a purpose to come out and take center stage in your life. She deserves her spotlight!

1. **How would you define your name?**

2. **And how will you commit to showing up as that person daily?**

A Moment To Reflect